THE POWER OF
POSITIVE
DRINKING

THE POWER OF POSITIVE DRINKING

CLEO ROCOS

EDITED BY SHARON MARSHALL

◙ SQUARE PEG

Published by Square Peg 2013

2 4 6 8 10 9 7 5 3 1

Copyright © Cleo Rocos 2013

Edited by Sharon Marshall

Designed by carrdesignstudio.com
Illustrations © Square Peg 2013

First published in Great Britain in 2013 by Square Peg
Random House, 20 Vauxhall Bridge Road, London SW1V 2SA

www.vintage-books.co.uk

Addresses for companies within The Random House Group Limited
can be found at: www.randomhouse.co.uk/offices.htm

The Random House Group Limited Reg. No. 954009

A CIP catalogue record for this book is available from the British Library

ISBN 9780224095679

The Random House Group Limited supports The Forest Stewardship
Council®(FSC®), the leading international forest certification organisation.
Our books carrying the FSC label are printed on FSC® certified paper. FSC is
the only forest certification scheme endorsed by the leading environmental
organisations, including Greenpeace. Our paper procurement policy can be
found at www.randomhouse.co.uk/environment

Printed and bound by CPI Group (UK) Ltd, Croydon, CR0 4YY

DEDICATION

To my fantastic family who I laugh uncontrollably with and absolutely love. Also to my fabulous friends. All these people magnificently star in the happiest highlights of my life.

For this book, I have taken the precaution, if not indeed the plunge on occasion, to discover the secrets of how to fully enjoy partying and cocktails without experiencing a hangover. It has taken years, but now my friends, I delight in being able to share with you, the key to *The Power of Positive Drinking*.... So here is to grabbing life by the cocktails and feeling fab the next day. Every great moment and celebration most definitely deserves to be remembered with a clear head.

'It's always too early to quit.'

Norman Vincent Peale, author, *The Power of Positive Thinking*

'Frankly I couldn't agree more, Norman.
I've been barking for a large one since noon.'

Cleo Rocos, author, *The Power of Positive Drinking*

UK GOVERNMENT GUIDELINES ON SENSIBLE DRINKING FOR ADULTS:

Men: 3–4 units per day
Women: 2–3 units per day

Well, that's the legal bit out of the way. And that's the only talk of 'units' that you'll find in this book. Personally, I find them all quite baffling, given that my knowledge of units is restricted to kitchen cupboards. And even I would feel the effect if I were to drink the contents of more than two of those at lunch.

This book is an explanation of mixology, not biology, so I won't accompany each recipe with stern words about the effects on the liver. If you ever perhaps think you're overdoing things a little party-wise, take a look at my Prehab chapter for guidance on throttling back or going alcohol free. Or there are excellent websites about responsible drinking such as www.drinkaware.co.uk.

CONTENTS

APERITIF

THE TWELVE STEPS TO THE LIQUID SIDE OF LIFE

This is not a self-help book. It's more a 'how to help yourself' book. But I've noticed a lot of those self-help scribes like to look to the spiritual side of life, have a little prayer or mantra or two. So let me do the same: *God grant me the wisdom to know the difference between good drinks and bad.*

Well, that's the whole point of this book. What I want you to be able to do is drink with maximum enjoyment and minimal grievous bodily harm. None of us want one of those dreadful hangovers where you wake up the next day and feel like a Krispy Kreme doughnut – gooey in the middle with crispy bits flaking off our outsides.

So, with my Positive Drinking mantra in mind, here are the twelve spiritual lessons on spirits and the rest of the drinks world. The twelve steps that will see you through the liquid side of life.

On the way, I'll throw in lots of recipes and tips for stain removal too.

All set? Let's go. I could murder a drink . . .

IN CASE OF EMERGENCIES

CHECK THE TIME, BREAK OPEN THE BOTTLE, KEEP CALM AND IMBIBE

Before we even start, there's a very important thing that we need to establish. Just when, exactly, is it OK to start drinking? There is, of course, a saying:

You should never drink before noon.

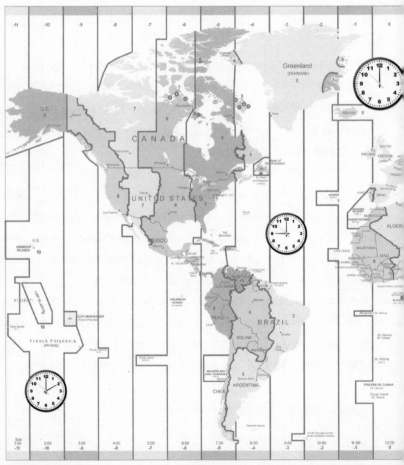

EASTWARD ACROSS DATE LINE ▶
subtract 24 hours

Not until the sun is over the yardarm, and all that.

Luckily, in my book, it's always noon somewhere.

In emergencies, and in case you've lost your inner compass, what better way of making sure that you're on the right side of the mainsail, than with this panoramic map of the world showing all its many time zones. Simply check the chart. See? Somewhere in the world, it is already noon. There's a shadow to be found over a yardarm on a boat somewhere on the high seas, so simply pull up a glass and dive in.

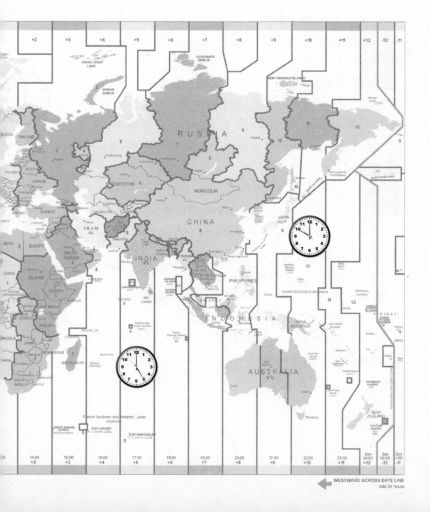

DRINKING ISN'T JUST FOR CHRISTMAS. IT'S FOR LIFE

This isn't a guide on how to get drunk. This is a guide to how to drink well.

This is a master class on how to drink and be merry: the secrets to avoiding hangovers, the recipes that bring you liquid sunshine from within and the science behind what to pour into a glass to ensure the most fabulous fun is had.

No one wants to wake up the next day feeling as though their head is in a small shoe.

I want to teach you how to drink successfully. How to reach that delicious level of intoxication where you and your fellow drinkers become the favourite versions of yourselves and stay there. How to ensure that every drinking occasion snowballs into a glorious and triumphant event.

Inside these pages lies the quintessence, the very spirit, if you like, of alcohol. The finest hints and tips on stylish drinking gleaned from a jolly crew of glorious people from around the globe. The odd recipe for some of the world's greatest drinks, along with a few of my own specialities, my signature tipples, which guarantee a quality night on the tiles, and a lot about how to have the right attitude for Positive Drinking.

All mixed, shaken and stirred with some tales about getting up to some happy trouble in the most unlikely places.

A WORD ON THE NAYSAYERS – OR THOSE WHO SAY NAY TO A DRINK.

Drinking has a bad reputation in some quarters. But I put it to you that the problem is neither alcohol nor drinking. No, what gives drinking a bad rap is simply people who are not doing it properly. A good-quality drink can bring all sorts and all types together and have a relaxing and positively joyous effect. Drink well and drink successfully and it can certainly take the stress out of a tough day.

Some of the greatest music, art, ideas and collaborations have been created whilst sipping on a glass of something alcoholic. Wars have been won, classic works written, beautiful romances have blossomed and lifelong friendships have been forged. A lot of us would not even be here today had our parents not indulged in a couple of cocktails or a bottle of champagne to help set the mood.

If you drink well, then drinking is simply a divine thing to do. It's a wonderful sensation. It lifts the spirits, soars the soul and lightens life. Everyone looks better, everyone seems funnier. Laughter abounds. The world is definitely a better place. What can possibly be wrong with that?

The greatest people enjoy a glass or two and are the better for it. I've had a headstand contest with Jack Nicholson, gone brothel-busting with Alan Carr, smuggled Princess Diana into drag bars and high-kicked to show tunes with Gore Vidal. It's all been glorious fun, but none of these gleeful events would have taken place if we hadn't got a drop of the proper stuff inside us.

I say proper stuff because *that's* the key to positive drinking. We've become obsessed with what we eat – organic this, five-a-day that –

but we know little and think even less about what we drink. Drink badly, and you'll get alcohol laden with chemicals, preservatives and sugar which cause wild mood swings, pile on excess poundage and leave you with a dreadful hangover.

Drink well and I promise you'll avoid all that.

Drinking should be a glamorous and stylish affair. Join me in discovering the fundamental rules that lead to a high-quality world of internal illumination.

LESSON ONE

THE ESSENTIAL DRINKS CABINET

There is no need to invest in expensive drinks equipment and you don't need any to make the simple recipes in this book.

Really the only thing I would recommend spending money on is your glasses. Alcohol tastes so much more expensive when served in a lovely glass and different alcohols behave differently so will benefit from being served in a glass that helps it reach perfection.

Encourage people to give them to you as presents: a nice set of large red-wine glasses that will give a beautiful wine some space; a set of crystal champagne flutes which will keep the sparkle of your bubbly; a lovely set of Martini glasses that can be adorned with an olive or a slice of lemon.

A nice glass is like putting a drink in its own little evening frock. It looks so much better and tastes so much more special. If you're throwing a party look at your local off-licences and see which will hire glasses for the event. Majestic Wine, for example, offer free glass loan and only charge £1 a glass for breakages.

Talking of breakages, really don't worry if glasses smash or if your glasses aren't all presented in perfectly matching sets. It's actually the height of chic to serve up drinks in mismatched glasses. If you're a party household then breakages are what happens, each missing glass tells a story of a glass that willingly gave its life in a kamikaze-fabulous party moment. Plus, having varying sizes of glassware enables you to slip the largest vessel in front of the guest you judge to be in most urgent need of liquid refreshment. Or throttle back with a smaller glass for someone who is teetering on being over-enthusiastic.

And never keep things for 'best'. Use the best all the time. Every drinking occasion should be a 'best' occasion. Personally, whenever I have a drink at the end of the day I like to draw a clear line separating work from play, by popping on a pair of diamond earrings, before settling back with an exquisite cocktail in an exquisite glass. A drink is a treat, a wonderful indulgence. It should be presented beautifully and respected.

But really that's the only equipment you need. A proper measuring jigger is invaluable but don't panic if you don't have one. For mixing and measuring you can invest in beautiful cocktail shakers if you wish, but there's no real need. Let me explain how with the first in my series of Frequently Asked Questions.

WHO GIVES A FAQ?

As I go through the book I've tried to answer the most commonly asked questions I receive when teaching people the art of alcohol: my very own FAQs.

A lot of the recipes in this book will list liquid measures in milliletres, usually abbreviated to mls. Or, for those of us brought up in the days of the imperial measure, 25ml is the same as 1 fl oz. This may all look very scientific but:

Do Not Panic

FAQ: I don't have measuring jugs and cocktail shakers, do I need all that to make the recipes work?

No. It's very simple. All the recipes in this book are based on single, 25ml shots.

If you wish, invest in a jigger to measure your shots, which you can pick up at a supermarket – they're only about a pound each, and make everything so much easier to measure.

Or you can measure using a shot glass. Here's a life-size illustration of a shot glass. A full glass is 50ml or a double shot, half is 25ml or a single shot.

50ml

40ml

30ml

20ml

10ml

0ml

If you don't have either of these handy don't worry.

Have a root around the medicine cabinet.

Ferret out the old bottle of cough mixture or some Night Nurse. They all come with a measuring cap with 25ml marked handily on the inside, so use that.

In terms of cocktail mixers, there's no need to spend hundreds on expensive silver shakers – though why not of course, if the mood takes you? Have a look on eBay or similar to sniff out a bargain. That said, I've worked with top mixologists at parties and watched them use old jam jars, coffee jars or Tupperware containers with a lid to shake things up in – they do the job just as well.

One tip: when I'm making a large amount of drink for a party I go to a kitchen shop and buy one of those industrial-sized plastic tomato-sauce dispensers (the sort you find in cafés) – they cost around £1 and make a cheap, perfect and jolly-shaped shaker.

ICE

One piece of essential equipment is your ice-cube tray.

There's absolutely no point spending all this time and money developing hand-selected cocktails, unadulterated by additives, sweeteners or colourings, with the best balance and taste, only for drinks to be marred by ice that is full of chlorine, fluoride and other chemicals found in tap water. It'll affect the taste.

Don't worry, it won't cost you a fortune to make your ice high quality. Just follow these rules.

NEVER use tap water. Use filtered or bottled still water for crystal-clear ice cubes that will not taint the taste of your drink. If your ice cubes are cloudy then the water is not pure.

NEVER use old ice cubes that have been sitting in your freezer for a while. The trays do not have a cover, and all the noxious compounds from your freezer edge their way in there and give the ice a musty taste. Freshen at least once a month.

GO LARGE: the bigger your ice cube the slower it melts. So if you want to add less water to your drink, and simply want to cool it, add large cubes. Buy the largest ice-cube trays you can find, fill with bottled water and freeze in advance. If you're catering for a large party you can buy huge ice cubes and balls at no great expense and have them delivered to your door by firms like www.eskimo-ice.co.uk.

Where I've called for a recipe to have crushed ice, there's no need for expensive ice-making machines: just take the ice cubes, put them in a carrier bag, or wrap in a clean dish cloth, and bash the outside about with a rolling pin to break them up.

And that's all you need.

So, now we've got all our equipment, it's about time we got on with the drinking. Cocktail, anyone?

FINDING THE HOLY GRAIL
(THE DRINKING CODE)

'Alcohol may be the road to nowhere,
but at least it's the scenic route.'
Bartender.com

'Well, let me take you on a journey through the cocktail
cabinet that's guaranteed NOT to leave you feeling carsick.'
Cleo Rocos

I'm about to make a big claim. The Holy Grail of drinking. The cocktail recipes in this book will not give you a hangover if you follow the recipes and the rules exactly. Yes. You read that right. Drink these divine cocktails and you will

PARTY HANGOVER-FREE.

It's up to you. Either skip straight to the recipes and get started or stay here and let's do the science bit.

THE SCIENCE BIT

Alcohol is the world's most popular recreational drug and, as will become abundantly clear in these chapters, I'm all in favour of good-quality products, consuming them with delight and knowing what and how to drink. But in order to understand why alcohol can cause havoc on the old head, let's look at what it does to the body.

The alcohol used in drinks is made by the fermentation of sugar using yeast. The result is an organic compound known as ethanol.

Settle down with your ethanol in a glass and have a sip, and it becomes absorbed through the stomach lining, enters the bloodstream, and then races round the body affecting various organs.

On the brain and central nervous system, the happy effect is to make us feel cheerful, sociable, euphoric and more confident. It makes everyone seem fabulous, it unclenches your thoughts, takes out all the corners and fills your head with warm ribbons of glee. On the skin it causes blood vessels to dilate causing a rise in temperature. The wonderful end result of both is a warm, surrendery feeling with your glass.

That's the good news. But there are other, less happy results to the body as the alcohol whirls round. Pump the body too full of alcohol and you start to struggle to walk straight as the tissue and fluids in the ears change and the ears are no longer able to give us a sense of balance.

Alcohol impacts kidney function. With each glass, the kidneys become less efficient at hanging onto and recycling water, thus leading to dehydration as water passes out of the body. And nausea and headaches can kick in as the liver starts to work at processing the alcohol. This is because the liver breaks down the alcohol using an enzyme called alcohol dehydrogenase (ADH), but the first stage of this breaking-down process converts the alcohol to a nasty chemical called acetaldehyde. Having this sloshing around inside you is what causes headaches and nausea until the body can break it down further and expel it. This is a hangover. You do not need to go through the pain of these unhappy stages. **A drunken whirling room and a hangover are a reminder that you haven't read this book properly.**

I am often asked how much is too much. It all varies from person to person. A lot of hangover resistance is down to biology. Men, for example, have more of the ADH enzyme than women so they can break down alcohol faster and 'hold' their drink better. Some East Asians have a mutation of the enzyme, which means they get drunk very quickly as they can't process it, but, as a general guide, the rather stylish science writer and chemist John Emsley has furnished me with this invaluable drinking barometer of the effects of alcohol on the average man. It comes from his award-winning book *The Consumer's Good Chemical Guide* which provides scientific guidance on the effect of chemicals on and in the body.

The effects of alcohol

Units	Number of drinks			Alcohol level in blood (mg per 100ml)	Effects on the average man*
	beer	**wine**	**spirits**		
2	1 pint	2 glasses	2 singles	30	feeling of well-being
3	1.5 pints	3 glasses	3 singles	50	lack of inhibitions
5	2.5 pints	5 glasses	5 singles	80	unfit to drive
6	3 pints	1 bottle†	6 singles	100	unsteady on feet
10	5 pints	1 litre	10 singles	150	slurring of speech
12	6 pints	2 bottles	½ bottle‡	200	drowsy and confused
18	9 pints	3 bottles	¾ bottle	300	drunken stupor
24	12 pints	4 bottles	1 bottle	400	dead drunk, maybe dying

* For a woman the same effects may be experienced with about two thirds the amount of alcohol that a man needs, assuming they are the same weight.

† Wines are traditionally sold in 700ml bottles.

‡ Spirits are often sold in bottles of 700ml, and this is what meant by a bottle here, not the 1 litre bottle which is becoming more common.

But it's not just the alcohol you have to watch out for. Other things will make a hangover worse: additives unscrupulous makers put in the bottle, ingredients that are perfectly legal but which you may be allergic to, and what's been put into whatever you choose to mix it with. All these can have a massive effect on your body's ability to process it. As English Physician Dr David Bull says: 'There are different purities of alcohol. The purer it is, the fewer side effects. If that wasn't bad enough, it's not just the alcohol that the body has to deal with. Many drinks have other things mixed in with them, including a lot of sugary colouring additives. We now know that pure alcohol causes far fewer symptoms than sweet sugary cocktails made with inferior alcohol.'

There are several myths out there about drinking: that if you stick to grape or grain you'll emerge unscathed; that if you drink a mix of drinks in a certain order – beer then wine – you'll 'be fine'; that you should avoid bubbles; avoid red wine or that throwing in a mixer like a cola will help.

None of these will actually work because they do not obey the rules of Positive Drinking.

What I've done in this book is consult a series of world experts to produce a list of recommendations that will help the body's chemical reactions to alcohol.

Follow my advice carefully and you should now have had your last hangover.

The brands listed and recommended throughout this book are some examples of the purest available versions of the drink, they are as additive-free as they can be, and have been made in the healthiest way possible to produce as few side effects as possible.

The cocktail recipes that I have listed are designed to be as pure and clean as possible, taking out anything that can rack up the pain, and suggesting alternatives that could actually speed up the metabolism process in the body and give a boost to that ADH enzyme that is working to break the alcohol down. The advice I've given on reading bottle labels is designed to enable you to sift the good from the bad, and spot at a glance which drinks are genuine quality products made with care, and which are charlatan products that will hit you the next day.

And where a drink is produced to a level of alcoholic strength that I feel is dangerously strong and the body would struggle to process it, I've suggested ways of bringing down its intensity, or at least furnished you with the knowledge of which drinks pack the greatest punch so you know to sip slowly with care.

And I'm not just here to save your head. Let me save your purse too. If there's a version or a brand of a drink that tastes just as good but is a fraction of the cost, I'll list it.

Oh, and, of course, they all taste fabulous too.

LESSON TWO

THE SKINNY ON SKINNY COCKTAILS

I f something is flavoured by a sweet, sticky sugar syrup or a sugary liquor it makes it harder for the body to process it. Sugary additives turn good spirits into evil ones.

1. *Sugar can cause massive mood swings*, sucking you into a vortex of depression.

2. *It piles on the pounds*. Sugared cocktails are high in calories. People tend to consume much more than they should because they are sweet, and start knocking them back at a pretty pace. Plus, a few glasses in and you'll be on such a sugar high that you'll feel an overpowering urge to lunge at the nearest food source and cram it all in. Sugar is the feeder of the drinking world. I've witnessed the politest of social circles suddenly becoming quite savage round the buffet after a couple of drinks.

So let's take the Classic Margarita and apply a little Positive spin to it.

THE CLASSIC MARGARITA
50ml tequila
25ml triple sec or Cointreau
150ml sweet and sour mix
Margarita salt
Fresh lime wedges

Pour all the ingredients into a cocktail shaker with ice,
salt the rim of the glass and then pour the mix, with ice, into each glass.
Garnish with the wedge of lime.

Now I'm not saying this drink tastes bad, in fact they can be utterly delicious. But if you make it like this you are drinking a headache and many more calories. **This recipe contains around 414 calories a glass.** Remember your last night on Margaritas? If the recipe was anything like this one, then I bet the room started to sway after about two. And you woke the next day with your tongue and half your brain stuck to the pillow.

Whatever you do, *do not serve this drink at parties*. You want your guests to recall with glee the amazing time they had. Not report that they can't remember a thing, woke up feeling as though their heads were clamped to a pneumatic drill and had to pull a sickie the next day.

So let's see what's wrong with it, and why it gives you such a cracking headache.

1. Firstly the mix of alcohol. You've got a liqueur AND a
    tequila. No wonder your head started to spin and Beelzebub
    was rampaging in your stomach and head the following day.

2. You've got a mouthful of salt – an old bartender's trick to give you a raging thirst that will send you scurrying to the bar for more and more. Just one glass rim can contain up to an entire day's recommended sodium allowance.

3. On top of all that, you've got sugar. Sugar in the triple sec, sugar in the sweet and sour mix, and sugar in some brands of tequila if you don't know what you're buying.

Right. Let's give that drink a positive, enlightening makeover.

THE POSITIVE DRINKING MARGARITA
50ml 100 per cent agave tequila
1–1½ limes, freshly squeezed
20ml organic agave syrup
Twist of orange peel
Wedge of lime

Take a piece of orange peel and squeeze that around the rim of the glass.

Fill a large tumbler with ice cubes to the rim. Put a large handful of ice cubes in a cocktail shaker. Add all the ingredients and shake fast and hard for five seconds or as soon as the shaker becomes wet and frosted on the outside. Pour into the glass of ice cubes but do not add the ice cubes from the shaker. Finish with a wedge of lime gently squeezed onto the Margarita and place on top of the ice in the glass.

This is incredibly simple to make. Just three ingredients. My six-year-old nephew can do it. Very successfully, may I add.

Anyway, child training aside, what have I done to make my Positive Drinking Margarita so marvellous?

1. **Why 100 per cent agave tequila?** If a bottle of tequila is marked 100 per cent agave tequila it is good and means it is not mixed with sugar-based alcohol derived from sugar cane distillation. Only ever drink 100 per cent agave tequila. It is made purely from the agave plant and, if consumed properly, will not give you a hangover. Yes, you read that correctly. You drink this glorious spirit and you'll be absolutely fine the next day and it only contains 64 calories per ounce. (See p91 where I'll recommend some of my favourite brands.)

2. **Use only one spirit.** By dropping the triple sec or Cointreau liqueur and instead adding organic agave syrup, which is a natural fructose, you swap the sugary liqueur for something that still gives that sweetness but is a slow-release carbohydrate with a low GI. Plus, by removing the liqueur you are also no longer mixing different alcohols in your glass. It's now just 100 per cent agave tequila.

3. **Why organic agave syrup?** Some agave syrups are organic but some are mixed with corn syrup, which contains sugar. The NON-organic agave syrup is not what you should choose or what I recommend at all. So when buying it make sure it only has one ingredient on the label and it should read, Organic Agave. In a blind judging in

2012, AquaRiva Organic Agave Syrup was voted to be the best quality by the *Spirits/Drinks Business* Magazine. You can find it online at thedrinkshop.com. The added benefit to this sweetener is that the high level of fructose it contains is known to help the body process alcohol.

4. **Why orange peel?** The Cointreau or triple sec liqueur gives the drink that delightful orange zesty hit, and the peel does the same job in a much nicer and benefit-enhancing way. Your nose will pick up the scent of fresh orange peel around the rim as you start to drink, and you get the pleasure, without the extra sugar or alcoholic hit of the Cointreau or triple sec.

5. **Why fresh limes?** By ditching the sweet and sour pre-mixed sugar-laden cocktail mix in favour of freshly squeezed limes, you lessen sugar content, which in turn prevents blood sugar levels swinging wildly off-beam. You also get a hit of vitamin C in each glass. Yet you still get that satisfying sour smack around the tongue against the sweetness of the agave. But once you start making your Margaritas with 100 per cent agave tequila, fresh limes and organic agave syrup, you will never want to have them any other way.

6. **This version of the Margarita contains 163 calories a glass.** Dropping all those sugary ingredients gives you a perfect fresh Margarita that tastes exquisite and so much more delicious. It also lessens calories. If on a night out when I'm expecting a few rounds, or if I'm serving at a

drinks party, I would personally lower the tequila shot to 35ml to ensure increased staying power for my guests, and this will taste just as delicious. Using a little less tequila and organic agave syrup also reduces the Margarita by 30 calories per drink.

7. **And as for the salt?** Just drop it. It might look pretty, but you'll get a much cleaner drink without it. Salt can dramatically interfere with the taste of your well-balanced Margarita and all it does is give you a raging thirst.

This drink tastes much better than the original with none of the side effects. It will not leave your tongue feeling as if it's coated in melted linoleum. You won't end up in the *National Enquirer* for bad behaviour after a mood swing. And, having served it up at hundreds of parties to A-list stars and VIPs, I guarantee your guests will adore it. It's absolutely delicious and a total triumph every time.

> 'One of the curious effects of a bad hangover is that you think you're wrong whether you are or not. Not wrong in particulars, but wrong in general, wrong about everything.'
> **Jim Harrison**

> 'The only thing wrong was your choice of drink. A hangover is the waste of a perfectly good day. And perfectly avoidable.'
> **Cleo Rocos**

THE STUFF THAT'S CHRONIC ABOUT TONICS

Let me give you another science lesson behind a brand recommendation. In the book I've been very specific about which brands of tonics you should use. Let me explain why.

In many instances where a spirit has a high alcoholic content – above 40 per cent ABV (alcohol by volume) – which I think could have a dangerously strong effect on the liver if consumed straight – I will recommend a mixer to go with it. This will make it a longer drink, giving your body more time to process each unit and stop you going into the danger areas of the drinking barometer.

As well as ensuring I recommend the best tasting brands, what I've also done is to go for the mixer that is as pure as possible – as sugar-free and additive-free as I can find. For example, with tonic waters I recommend three great brands for UK drinkers: Waitrose own-label, Fever-Tree and Fentimans.

The reason why is that if you're choosing a diet or slimline version of a tonic to lessen the impact of a drink on your waistline, then they can often contain **aspartame** – the controversial artificial sweetener. There are several claims on the internet of what it's said to do. I won't go into hysteria-mongering here, but given the choice, I personally would absolutely avoid it completely. It is present in several major brands.

So if you're looking for a low-calorie tonic, then check the label carefully and see if it is present, or if a more natural flavouring has been used. Let me go through my favourites:

Fever-Tree Particularly its Naturally Light Tonic Water, which is light in calories, and is flavoured with pure fructose instead of aspartmane.

Waitrose Tonic Water Its sugar-free version is excellent. This tonic is also the best I've found for keeping its sparkle.

Fentiman's Tonic Water A light, lower calorie tonic water, continuing the company ethos of using fine natural ingredients. Amazon delivers this in packs of twelve.

All combine beautifully with a gin or vodka and are free from any nasties that are going to crank up your hangover in the morning.

This theory of eradicating nasties is the theme I've used throughout the book. Let's go back to those drinking myths.

It's fine to drink bubbles and champagne, but only if you choose a champagne that's as pure as possible.

You can emerge after a night on red wine unscathed, but only if you know how to read the bottle to ensure its contents have been produced by as natural and additive free a way as they can be.

Sticking to one type of alcohol all night works, but only if you're drinking the same, pure, healthily mixed drink that contains none of the nasties. Otherwise, mix or not, you're on that bobsleigh to hell.

Anyway, that's the science. Drinking positively is all about drinking with maximum enjoyment, but minimal impact on your body, purse and your dignity.

In each chapter I'll list the best and worst of what's out there. But meanwhile here's an at-a-glance guide to what to put in your glass. Like the periodic table, some elements are distinctly unstable and so will you be if you drink them.

THE PERIODIC TABLE OF DRINKING

Cm
Any cocktail made in a machine

Rp
Rum punch

Sa
Sangria

Ges
Export Strength Gin

Mw
Mulled wine

Wo
Wine at office parties

Ab
Absinthe

Bc
Blue Curaçao

Af
Anything from Faliraki

Gr
Grappa

Ag
Anything green

Ad
Anything containing a dead animal

Pg
A Pan Galactic Gargle Blaster*

Avoid

Not so noble gases

Ch
Champagne

Fw
Fizzy water

Fj
Fruit Juices

Avoid at all costs
Especially on a plane

One Glass

Co
Any drink mixed with cola

Bw
Any wine served from a box

Nb
Something your neighbour brewed

Ss
Any cocktail containing sugar syrup

Ao
Anything over 40%ABV

Cr
Anything containing Cream

Tn
Any tequila not marked 100% agave

Two Glasses

Ru
Unfiltered rum

Ap
Anything served on a plane

Vm
Vodka Martini

Gm
Gin Martini

Sc
Sweet champagne

Ws
Whiskey Sour

Po
Port

Three Glasses

Ow
Organic wine

Bw
Biodynamic wine

Wm
whisky mizuwari

Fr
Filtered aged rum

Dc
Dry champagne

Ub
Ultra Brut champagne

Party Night!

Ta
100% agave tequila

Gs
Gin and sugar free tonic

Vs
Vodka and sugar free tonic

Pc
Any positve cocktail in this book

Gc
Anything with Grand Cru on the front

---

* I drank one of these in the original TV series of The Hitchhiker's Guide to the Galaxy, died instantly and turned into steam. Best avoided

LESSON THREE

THE VLODDY MARVELLOUS THINGS ABOUT VODKA

'If life gives you lemons, you should make lemonade.'
Anon

'Actually, if life gives you a lemon, I would strongly advise reaching for a bottle of vodka and a splash of vermouth and making yourself a lovely Martini with a twist.'
Cleo Rocos

We may as well start with the hard stuff, and vodka, if handled correctly, can be vloddy marvellous. It contains only 64 calories per 25ml, is totally free of carbohydrates and yet has the kick of a mule after a long day.

Going back to the idea of spiritual pointers and pointing you to a higher power and all that sort of thing: would it help if I told you that legend has it that vodka was invented by a monk?

THE HISTORY OF VODKA:
A spiritual story

According to legend, vodka was created by a Greek chap called Isidor. Isidor was part of a Russian delegation to Florence in 1438. The delegation also visited Venice where he was introduced to distillation techniques. On his return to Moscow, following some imprudent statements, Isidor was confined to the Chudov Monastery inside the Kremlin and it is said that it is there that he came up with the recipe for the hard stuff, making this first Russian vodka from grain. Having perfected his tipple, he plied his guards with vodka, got them drunk, then escaped to Rome, leaving behind his distilling instruments.Clearly he become a bit of a hero with the Russians, who took this as a 'sign', made vodka the national drink, stuck his name in the history books and his invention in their cocktail cabinets, and have knocked the stuff back like mother's milk ever since.

WHAT SORT OF VODKA CAN I DRINK POSITIVELY?

The bad news about vodka is that there's an awful lot of rough stuff out there. And you can end up spending an absolute fortune in bars as barmen try to steer you towards what they say is the good stuff.

People drink vodka with their eyes. I don't mean they literally pour it into their orbits, although I did hear of someone trying this once at a party and apparently they were carted off, weeping, to the first-aid cabinet. I mean they buy something and claim something is their favourite brand purely because they've fallen for a marketing campaign.

According to the marketing, there are vodkas out there with superior purity or taste, or with the ability to make you look like an absolute Sex God or Goddess with the power to make the object of your desire go all warm and surrendery just at the sight of you sipping from a glass of it.

Do not fall for this hype.

In fact, let me get you the cost of this book back in just one round, by explaining why there's no point paying for an expensive vodka in a bar.

No doubt a vodka aficionado would scream at me for saying this, but, in my opinion by the time a vodka has been mixed with other ingredients you would truly have to possess a magnificently professional set of taste buds to be able to tell which brand you're being served and tell the difference between a value brand and a premium one. In fact, in one blind taste test, five out of six people could not pick out their favourite premium vodka from a line-up.

The thing with the vodka that is generally served is that it can be distilled up to five times, which means that there is very little or no flavour left, and then most vodkas are mixed with water before bottling, plus it tends to be served ice cold.

Now, always be wary of any alcohol that MUST be consumed ice cold. It's often a sign that it's made from inferior ingredients with a flavour that you could not swallow at room temperature. A great vodka should be perfectly drinkable at room temperature (even if you wouldn't actually, if you see what I mean). Through chilling, bad flavour is disguised and that's why some ad campaigns will only advertise their brand to be served ice cold. But once highly chilled or if you shove it in a cocktail with other mixers or juices, it is virtually impossible to tell the difference between the vodka brands. So if it's your round, or if you're throwing a party with cocktails, I'd say go for a 'quality' value vodka – see my recommended list of good brands below – and save your cash. It's only if you're on a date, or throwing a party at home and wish to impress, that it's worth buying the top brands.

This is not to say that all vodkas are equal. When out shopping, if you don't recognize the brand, a good way of telling if it's a good vodka is to look at the label and see what it's been made from. Vodka can be made from anything - grains, potatoes, fruits, old socks – look for brands made with winter wheat and rye. This will show that they have been made from a superior grain. Having said that, I can recommend a great quality potato vodka for you too. Go for a Polish vodka if you want a smoother and more flavourful drink. Go for a Russian one if you like a drink that gives you an almighty smacker and then dances around your chops before shrieking 'hello' and dragging you out for a party.

QUALITY 'VALUE' VODKAS

This is by no means an exhaustive list. But these are the brands that have been recommended to me as good 'value' brands from respected bartenders around the world who are happy to serve them to their customers. Put any of these in your cocktail and you're going to be doing OK by your head and not breaking the bank. If, when ordering your drink the barman looks at you and asks: 'bartender's choice?', say no. Instead scan the shelves, see if you can find one of these brands, and ask for it. I find that smiling and adding: 'Mind you, I expect you'll serve it so cold that I won't be able to taste it anyway,' usually results in a smile from the barman, and a little extra effort from him over the ice shaker.

I have served these up to vodka aficionados who swear blind they have a favourite, premium vodka, and all of them have pronounced it delicious.

Finlandia Vodka

Ketel One Vodka

Vodka Wyborowa

Blavod Black Vodka

Russian Standard Vodka

SKYY Vodka

There are, of course, some complex vodkas that can be sipped and savoured at room temperature and are worth the extra:

Chase Vodka

Konik's Tail Vodka

Sipsmith Vodka

Vestal Vodka

Sacred Vodka

Belvedere Vodka

Time for another Frequently Asked Question. This is a guidebook after all. I'm here to serve. Or at least help you serve up.

FAQ: How much vodka should I drink?

'The first glass of vodka goes down like a post, the second like a falcon and the third like a little bird.'
Old Russian Saying

I perhaps wouldn't ask the average Russian for advice on vodka consumption. Vodka's name stems from the Russian word 'voda', meaning water. And they drink about the same amount of both. In fact, Emperor Peter the Great was said to get through an impressive 2 litres a day.

I'd say take it slightly easier. Vodka is a deceptive drink. It's ghost in colour, it's transparent, it looks quite innocuous. But it can pack a hefty punch. Vodka usually contains at least 38 per cent ABV and can sell at up to 88 per cent ABV.

I don't really enjoy or recommend spirits over 40 per cent ABV as there is far too much alcohol content for my liking and health. Serve it as a straight vodka Martini for example and it's like a hypodermic syringe going into your veins. Like Sharon Stone in *Basic Instinct*, high-alcohol-content vodkas look all innocent and cool, but they'll come and whack you over the back of the head. And before you know it, you are out of control and devoid of a full complement of undergarments.

If drinking it as a Martini, or straight, try not to drink anything over 38 per cent ABV, if drinking it long, I'd really avoid anything over 40 per cent ABV.

A vodka Martini, if prepared properly, is going to be incredibly strong. So when it comes to how many vodka Martinis you should drink in one sitting, I say they're like broken marriages:

One is utterly understandable. Two really is quite enough. And once you start getting to three and beyond, people are going to start talking about you.

That's not to say I don't recommend them. They're a marvellous warm-up drink, a precursor to fun, or an instant hit after a troublesome day.

I remember the night I discovered Martinis. It involved Jack Nicholson, Bruce Willis and an Argentinean Tango dance troupe . . .

MY FIRST MARTINI NIGHT

There was this amazing bar in downtown Los Angeles called Helena's. It had little slit windows right at the top of these 20-foot walls so no one could see in, and it was run by a striking, feisty Greek woman by the name of Helena who only let you in if she liked the look of you. Now one thing she really liked the look of was Hollywood A-listers and they would all go and party there, safe from marauding photographers. Which is just as well because the night I went involved a headstand competition with Jack Nicholson.

The night started gloriously, with Madonna drinking Martinis with Bruce Willis. (Bruce, incidentally, is an

ex-barman and mixes a mean vodka Martini cocktail
so this choice of drink was all his idea.) Jack Nicholson
swaggered in for the night along with *Godfather* legend
Robert Duvall and the divine Princess Stephanie, who,
like the rest of us, was in proper trim and ready to party.
Down went the first round.

Next, the Tango Argentina troupe popped in and
Robert Duvall turned out to be a bit of a Tango fanatic
and dragged me onto the floor for a dance. He's fabulous
on the dance floor. There was one hairy moment when
he just fell completely backwards and everyone thought
he had died, but he just got up, laughed and carried
on. Which I always think is absolutely the best way
to deal with any temporary paralysis through cocktail
dehydration.

In what was quite a lively night, I remember that
Princess Stephanie almost set the club on fire after
throwing a lit cigarette in the bin. It was all fine, though,
and various Hollywood types came over to watch, and
calmly lit their cigarettes from the blaze before it was
safely extinguished. We then returned, shrieking with joy,
to the bar.

At this point I was two Martinis in, and really, most
definitely warmed up for a night of happy trouble. Which
is as well because at around about 3 a.m. Jack Nicholson
sidled over with one of those illegally mischievous smiles

that make you completely fall under his spell. He wanted to do a headstand competition. Of course I agreed. He then insisted we started drinking shots upside down whilst we did it. I agreed to that, too. Because he does have a very good smile.

With a little assistance from a couple of Hollywood stars who were looking on, I popped myself upside down in my tight cocktail dress, stayed up there for a bit and managed to pour the shot up my nose. Jack fared much better and managed to stay upside down for a good while, downing shots to general applause from the assembled troops. I have the feeling he may have done it before.

The whole evening only ended sometime around 4 a.m. when Jack's girlfriend persuaded him to turn the right way up again and get into a cab.

THE PERFECT MARTINI?

Every bartender will give you a different variation on this (olives, twists, shaken, stirred, and all that). I'd say there's no harm in trying out a few different variations – all in the interests of research, of course. Like a box of chocolates, if you don't like one particular combination, you can always try another. And if you like it, have another just to be sure.

But here is a pretty failsafe recipe for a perfect Martini just like the ones we drank on the night Jack took my Martini virginity.

A Martini is one of those drinks that braces you up and prepares you for the night ahead. This version is perfect for doing headstands with Hollywood stars.

DRY MARTINI (MAKES ONE)
50ml good vodka (max 40 per cent ABV)
Two teardrops of a dry Vermouth such as Noilly Prat
A sliver of lemon peel

Keep your vodka in the freezer. Pour the frozen vodka into a cocktail shaker – 50ml of vodka for every person – and just two drops of dry Vermouth per person. Shake and pour, adding a sliver of lemon peel to the glass.

Vermouth, incidentally, is merely there as a fragrance. It is just a touch to enhance what is basically a neat vodka. I cringe when I see people put in a whole shot.

Drink this version anyway up you please. But please note that upside down takes practice.

Do you need help on slivering your lemon?

THE PERFECT LEMON SLIVER

1. Using a knife or potato peeler cut a thin oval from an unwaxed lemon. You want this oval to be about 2.5cm in length and as thin and with as little white pith as possible.
2. Twist this peel over your finished Martini, peel side down so citrus oil is dispersed into the drink.
3. Rub the peel around the rim of the glass before throwing it into your Martini.

If you want a pretty ribbon of peel, then just take a thin slice of lemon, remove the fruit and then twist the rind into a spiral, or invest in a lemon zester and cut a spiral from your lemon working from the top down. But the method above gives you a better tasting drink as the lemon oil adds aroma and flavour to your Martini.

FAQ: Is there any dress code for drinking vodka positively?

'Why don't you slip out of those wet clothes and into a dry Martini?'
Robert Benchley

One thing I learned from that evening with Jack is that vodka does tend to lead you deliciously into a night of happy trouble. With that in mind, ladies, I'd say you should always go out cocktailing in a skirt that reaches below the knee, as you never quite know what's going to happen.

It will help you look modest even if you find yourself happily swinging from a chandelier. And do at all times wear a full complement of underpinnings, please. There is nothing ladylike in displaying a honeymoon pout.

A delightful thing about vodka is that it doesn't stain anything when spilt. In fact, it can be used as a makeshift dry cleaner in emergencies (see below) so feel free to drink the stuff in your finest attire.

FAQ: How should I store my vodka?

'Always do sober what you said you'd do drunk.
That will teach you to keep your mouth shut.'
Ernest Hemingway

Despite what I've said above about what freezing does to flavour, as most vodkas have hardly any, at home you should always keep your vodka bottle in the freezer – it will then always be at the perfect temperature for mixing cocktails without needing all that faffing about shaking it over ice cubes in a cocktail maker. Even if it's good vodka, it's always going to do a better job in your cocktails cold. The bit about drinking it at room temperature is to make sure that it's drinkable at all. To make it pleasurable, you want to make it freezing cold, enabling you to pour instant delicious icy-cold Martinis.

Do always make sure you screw the top of the vodka bottle back on as spirits can evaporate otherwise. (However, this 'evaporation' can always be used as a handy excuse, when questioned, to explain any depleted supplies.)

FAQ: Is there anything that can make bad vodka better?

'Money, like vodka, turns a person into an eccentric.'
Anton Chekhov

Well, the simple answer is no. Whereas a decently mixed cocktail can turn a decent value brand into an absolute high-end triumph, there is little you can do if you receive a gift of a vodka that appears to be made from old socks, takes the roof of your mouth off, and tastes like petrol.

Don't drink the scoundrel. But don't throw it out either. Here are my top tips for how to make the best use of it.

Flowers Add a few drops of vodka to the vase water along with one teaspoon of sugar and the blooms will live longer and smell sweeter. Change the water every other day, refreshing the vodka/sugar each time. NB: If you've had a bad day and are drinking alone then 'sharing' your vodka with your flowers in this way does not count as 'company'.

Dry Cleaning Vodka is a brilliant dry cleaner. Keep a few shots in a spray bottle. It kills odour caused by bacteria, but doesn't leave a scent when dry. If you're left with less-than-fragrant armpits in a well-loved item of clothing, simply spray the spot and then leave it to dry. (Of course, I would never suggest you try to hoodwink a store like some naughty teenager by wearing clothes out for a night and then spraying them and returning them claiming they're unworn. I simply wish to point out that this dry-cleaning method goes completely undetected and will not leave your clothes smelling like an air freshener dangling in a minicab. This is a hot tip from the fashion experts.)

HOW WELL ARE YOU DOING?
THE POSITIVE VODKA-DRINKING QUIZ

I want us all to drink responsibly, so do ask that perhaps at some point you run through these quiz questions. I just want to make sure you're not at Peter the Great levels of consumption. (If you are, maybe check out Lesson 12, p197 – my Prehab section.)

What time do you have your first vodka?

☐ Pre dinner Correct.

☐ Pre breakfast Oh dear. Well, unless you're still up from last night . . .

How was your last vodka served?

☐ In a Martini How very nice.

☐ Long, in a Bloody Mary Big night, was it? Incidentally, for a perfect Bloody Mary recipe see p40

☐ Straight out of the flower vase Oh dear.

☐ In a shot glass, upside down in the middle of a roaring crowd Ah, hello again, Mr Nicholson. How's it all going?

MORE VLODDY MARVELLOUS PRESCRIPTIONS

Here are some recipes that I have gleaned from some of the world's friendliest barmen about how to mix the healthiest versions of popular vodka cocktails.

Think of these as your Positive Drinking medicine bag while you get better acquainted with Dr Drink as he does the rounds of the Hospitality Ward. You'll soon build up a repertoire that'll make you the most intensively caring and popular host.

'Vodka is our enemy, so we'll utterly consume it!'
Russian proverb

BLOODY MARY
25ml vodka
5ml dry sherry
2 dashes Angostura®
aromatic bitters
50ml tomato juice
10ml freshly squeezed
lemon juice
6 drops Tabasco sauce
10ml Worcestershire sauce
½ teaspoon horseradish sauce
GLASS: Highball
GARNISH: Ground pepper and celery stick

Shake all ingredients together and strain into your glass.
Add pepper and garnish with a fresh and crunchy celery stick.

MOSCOW MULE

50ml Vodka

25ml freshly squeezed
lime juice

4 dashes Angostura®
aromatic bitters

Fever Tree ginger beer

GLASS: Highball

GARNISH: Lime wedge and a sprig of mint

Build over cubed ice, top up with ginger beer

DUSK IN EDEN

35ml vodka

1 large slice of pomegranate, chopped

25ml apple juice

5ml organic agave syrup

Pomegranate seeds to garnish

GLASS: Martini glass

Muddle the pomegranate and organic agave syrup in a mixing glass or
shaker. Add vodka, apple juice and ice to the shaker and shake well.
Strain into a chilled Martini glass. Garnish with pomegranate seeds.

WILD BERRY CAIPIROSKA
50ml Finlandia Wild Berries vodka
20ml organic agave syrup
30ml freshly squeezed lime juice
4 fresh raspberries
4 fresh blackberries
2 fresh lime wedges
GLASS: Lowball (rocks)

With a muddler or wooden spoon, muddle three of each berry and lime
wedges in a rocks glass and then strain the muddled berries into a
cocktail shaker. Add the organic agave syrup, fresh lime juice
and vodka. Fill the rocks glass with crushed ice. Shake the cocktail
shaker vigorously for five seconds, pour in the glass
and garnish with fresh berries.

LESSON FOUR

HOW TO REIGN WITH CHAMPAGNE

*'I only drink champagne when I'm happy and when
I'm sad. Sometimes I drink it when I'm alone. When I have
company I consider it obligatory. I trifle with it if I'm not
in a hurry and drink it when I am, otherwise I never
touch the stuff unless I am thirsty.'*
Lily Bollinger

*'Well, Lily, the first three obviously didn't touch the sides . . .
Glass of bubbly, anyone?'*
Cleo Rocos

Oh champagne! It's impossible for anyone to stay cross when they're handed that first glass of champagne. Trust me, it's got me out of trouble on many, many occasions.

It's a party drink. The elixir of celebration. The Lourdes of a tipple – drink it and be cured of any unhappiness. The bubbles in the glass seem to leap up through the surface and turn that little frown upside down.

Like a flute of liquid diamonds. A glass of Hollywood smiles. The choice of royalty. That's how champagne is marketed. Which is very clever, actually, because if you don't drink it properly you end up feeling distinctly rough and supremely un-regal.

On to how to choose and serve it in a moment. And how some really sophisticated people don't just drink it in on its own, but mix it with the most delicious things. Which reminds me of the day Princess Diana introduced me to peach Bellinis – and what happened next . . .

MY BEST BELLINI

There was always a great excitement and anticipation after receiving an invitation for a gleeful lunch with Princess Diana. She was a big fan of the *Kenny Everett Show* and we got to know each other over the years. She had a happily wicked sense of humour. We would meet and the three of us would swap all the fabulous gossip and the goings-on.

On one such occasion we met for lunch at The Bombay Brasserie in Kensington. She arrived smiling and was clearly looking forward to a jolly lunch. There were no bodyguards visible at all.

I had been toying with the idea of a Kir Royale but Diana suggested that we should all have a peach Bellini [a divine cocktail made with champagne and peach juice] instead as she said that they made 'A good one here'. So we did, and she was right.

Within moments we were chatting madly. Diana loved hearing about which stars and celebrities were doing what behind the scenes with whom and who was 'really gay'. We would tell her all the hottest showbusiness news and she would tell us the palace gossip and we'd all shriek with laughter.

She would often refer to someone by their star sign, saying 'Oh that randy old Taurean' or 'Typical Sagittarean, always dancing on the table with a bottle of vodka down his trousers'.

To this day, the secrets traded round that table have never been made public. But there are some Taureans and Sagittareans who are very lucky the newspapers don't follow them more closely.

The glorious thing about Diana is that she did enjoy a good laugh and those Bellinis did go down well with all of us.

That afternoon, we all went back to watch *The Golden Girls* at Kenny's penthouse up the road.

Upon entering his flat, the first thing Diana did was kick off her shoes. Kenny had a collection of feather dusters that looked like an explosion of exotic dancing girls in the corner of his living room. I went into the kitchen to make champagne cocktails only to return to find Diana and Kenny dancing to the Gypsy Kings, waving the feather dusters in wafts of sheer delight.

That evening Kenny and I had plans to go out for drinks with Freddie Mercury who lived only inches away up the road and was also a great chum.

Kenny phoned Freddie and told him to come over early as Diana was here and we were going to watch *The Golden Girls*. I don't think that anything could get more camp than Diana, Kenny, Freddie and I sitting on Kenny's sofa all watching *The Golden Girls*. Kenny turned the sound down on the television and we all improvised the voices but with a much naughtier storyline. Kenny was Blanche, Diana was Dorothy, Freddie was Sophia and I was Rose. I daren't tell you the plot we gave them but it was magnificently debauched and wildly camp and we were uncontrollable with laughter. Diana was giggling from behind a cushion and asked what our plans were for that evening. Freddie told her that we were going to the Vauxhall Tavern – a rather notorious gay bar in London.

Diana said that she had never heard of it and she'd like to come too.

Now this was not a good idea. 'It's not for you,' said Kenny. 'It's full of manly hairy gay men. Sometimes there are fights outside.' This didn't put her off in the slightest. 'What would the headline be if you were caught in a gay bar brawl?' we pleaded.

But it was clear that Diana was in full mischief mode and turned to Freddie. He loved it and was always up for pushing the boundaries. 'Go on, let the girl have some fun. Can you IMAGINE?' he said, unable to keep his huge smile from turning to laughter.

She just wanted the thrill of going in, undetected, to order one drink, and would then leave right away, she promised. By this point she had tried on the outfit Kenny had intended to wear – a camouflage army jacket, hair tucked up into a leather cap and dark aviator sunglasses. Scrutinizing her in the half-light we decided that the most famous icon of the modern world might just . . . JUST, pass for a rather eccentrically dressed gay male model.

Half an hour later we were all in the cab arriving at the Vauxhall Tavern.

Kenny went in first, very closely followed by me then the cross-dressing Diana, with Freddie right behind her. The bar was full. It took an absolute aeon to edge our way to the bar, with person after person cheerfully greeting us. It was fabulously outrageous and so bizarrely exciting.

Our hearts pounded with every new leather-clad hairy body that approached, but no one, absolutely no one, recognised Diana.

On we inched, through the leather throngs and thongs, until finally we reached the bar. We were nudging each other like naughty school children, Diana and Freddie were giggling, but she did order a white wine and a beer. Once the transaction was completed we all looked at one another, united in our triumphant quest. We did it! Never has going to a bar been quite so exhilarating and fun. We then made a swift exit, a cab was hailed and we whisked Diana back to Kensington Palace. The jolly queens queuing outside the bar unknowingly waved back as their Queen of Hearts waved goodbye to them. Not a single person ever found us out.

The next day Diana sent the outfit back to Kenny's flat with a lovely handwritten thank-you note to us all ending with the words: We must do it again!

I've had many a Bellini since and they always lead to joyous mischief. Should you ever be faced with a beautiful Princess wanting an illicit night out I find they are the very thing. Here's how to make them:

PEACH BELLINIS (MAKES TWO)

Two ripe peaches, peeled, halved and stone removed, or if you have to, tinned peaches in natural juice (not syrup)

Chilled dry champagne or sparkling wine

Blend the peaches in a blender and put two tablespoon of the peach purée into a chilled champagne glass. Top up the glass with champagne, stirring as you pour.

Diana never drank a lot, and we'd never drink much when we were all out together. We'd drink just enough to get us into happy trouble for the evening and to be able to remember it all. Peach Bellinis – a half-and-half of fruit juice and crisp champagne – are a lovely, clean way of stretching out the alcohol fun over an afternoon.

Plus, they tell me that peaches contain vitamins A and C, potassium, calcium, magnesium, phosphorus and folate. I'm not even sure what the last few things are. But apparently they're all good. And I do know they left us all with a peachy glow of happiness that afternoon.

So that is champagne on a good day. Drink it like this, in moderation, in good company, over food and with joy, and it's delightful. But get it wrong and it can give you a most horrific hangover. And a shocking bill. Let me tell you about how good champagne can go bad.

WHEN GOOD CHAMPAGNE GOES BAD

Champagne is like a supermodel: utterly beautiful, but terribly expensive and capable of quickly turning evil.

It can also be a total charlatan when it comes to quality.

Firstly, champagne is one of those alcohols that is always served very chilled, which makes it harder to taste whether you are getting a superior product or not. Inferior champagne makers are able to further mask any product deficiencies behind a wall of sugar, which is added to create fermentation so that it becomes fizzy and more palatable and exciting. Then comes the trusty trick of serving it from a bottle with a fabulous label and packaging. And years of marketing have convinced us that indulging in this effervescent liquid at great speed and in great quantities is a sign of glorious affluence and joy, not foolhardiness. The marketing around champagne is sheer genius. Personally I do not believe there is any product anywhere that is better marketed. Ask yourself this. When was the last time you drank champagne at room temperature? And if you did, how did you like the taste? Hmmm . . . I thought so.

So, as with vodkas, I'll list a few failsafe brands that won't break the bank or your head when you have that need to celebrate with your friends, and sparkling wines that will do a particularly good job if you're adding a dash of peach or something else to them to put you in the pink.

Spain:

Cava – made primarily in Catalonia and usually displaying aromas and flavours of green apple and citrus.

The Cava Houses of Freixenet and Codorníu produce an impressive range of sparkling wines, from value-wines to premium examples.

A couple of examples from each house (prices are approximate):

Freixenet Cordon Negro, Brut Cava (£9.00)

Freixenet Elyssia Gran Cuvée,Cava Brut (£16.00)

Bach Brut Nature, Cava (£8.00)

Codorníu Reina Maria Cristina, Blanc de Noirs Cava (£15.00)

Italy:

Prosecco – the in-vogue sparkling wine with its characteristic peachy aromatic quality is used extensively in cocktails as well as a refreshing aperitif in its own right.

Some of the mass-produced versions can be a little bland, but this is true in many sparkling wine producing areas around the world.

A couple to look out for:

Fabiano Prosecco Castello 4357 Brut NV (£10.00)

Giavi Brut - Prosecco Superiore Valdobbiandene DOCG (£15.00)

France:

Limoux, just south of Carcassonne in the Languedoc-Roussillon region of South-West France, produces excellent but under-valued sparkling wine. Delicate green apple and floral notes are its characteristic traits.

Blanquette de Limoux, Château Rives-Blanques (£14.00)

LET'S GET THE PARTY STARTED

There is one crucial rule to remember to successfully serve champagne at a party and to ensure that your guests are as hangover-free as possible the next day. It is the Rule of Feet.

THE RULE OF FEET

Think about how your guests will be at your party.

Will they be sitting down at a table? Or on their feet?

If they are going to be on their feet then **never ever** serve champagne for an entire party or you're putting them firmly on a bobsleigh to Hell. Here's why.

SERVING CHAMPAGNE AT PARTIES (STANDING UP)

The problem with champagne is that it comes in its own special glass. A tall, thin, elegant glass. It's a glass of aspirations. Just holding it makes you feel expensive and chic. It implies that you are in the right place with the right people and literally drinking in the wealth. Just like the glass, you feel thin, long and elegant, which is all extremely enchanting, apart from one thing. **People never, ever want to let go of their aspirational glass. And they hate to see it empty.** People cling onto their glasses protectively. They panic if they see it's running out. They drink quicker as it starts to lose its cold crisp edge.

Watch closely at parties, and you'll see that the most stylish of people teeter on becoming quite shirty and protective of their champagne flute. They will cling onto that glass all night, plaintively holding it out to every passing waiter, never letting it run empty.

Of course, everyone knows they should have a glass of water in between each glass, but they don't. Water needs a different glass. It means putting the special champagne glass down. Risking it being cleared. Risking never getting another one. Risking not being able to get any more champagne that night. So instead, as the waiter comes round with a champagne bottle, they go for the refill and drink some more.

Everyone knows they should eat at these functions, too. But people don't. You don't want to be standing there holding chicken bones. With no knife and fork, guests don't want to end up with sticky fingers and stained garments or with puff-pastry crumbs all round their chops and décolletage. And dressed in their tight fitting dresses, ladies are often self-conscious about their stomachs – out on display instead of safely hidden beneath a tablecloth, so they tend not to eat much. Instead, they just keep drinking the champagne.

Four hours later, no one has any idea how much they've consumed, they've not had a sip of water and barely a mouthful of food all night and they're a hot mess hurtling towards a kaleidoscopic stinker of a hangover.

Oh, and that's not all that can be stinking. Do bear in mind that this bubbliest of drinks can, if knocked back too quickly, lead to an absolutely devastating build up of fermenting gas inside you. One unfortunate woman who drank a little too much at a party will forever be known in London circles as 'Hovercraft Hetty'. Let's just say that she produced so much steam during one evening's drinking, the build-up was such that the guests were shocked into silence as she gave way to such an earth-shattering emission from her skirts, that her feet were no longer touching the floor.

Oh dear.

Think of champagne like foie gras. A delicious treat. But if it's all you serve, everyone will become sick on it. Personally, other than perhaps a glass for a toast, I never drink or serve just straight champagne at a party where everyone's on their feet. Instead, you should go for low-sugar cocktails topped with champagne and served in a long glass. It makes everyone a lot happier and would have saved Hovercraft Hetty her awkward social blushes.

Here are some Positive Drinking recipes to serve at stand-up parties.

CHAMPAGNE PARTY PRESCRIPTIONS

These will actually cost less than serving straight champagne and will leave all guests feeling fresh and perky the next day.

Elderflower, Skinny Tequila and Champagne cocktails

This drink is absolutely perfect for weddings. It's a summer's day in a glass. Accordingly, I've given quantities for 100 guests, with three cocktails assumed for each guest. This works out much, much less costly than serving champagne all night, will be delightfully decadent, and easier on everybody's heads and bodies.

FOR 100 GUESTS

10 bottles of champagne

12 bottles of Reposado 100 per cent agave tequila

8 500ml bottles of elderflower cordial

13 350ml bottles of organic agave syrup

900 raspberries (3 per cocktail)

300 sprigs of mint (1 sprig per cocktail)

Hire out tall glasses from your local liquor and wine store and prepare the elderflower and agave mixes in advance. Into each glass pour one shot of tequila, one shot of elderflower cordial and 15ml agave syrup. Add the three raspberries and a sprig of mint. You can easily have 100 glasses of this prepared in advance. As each guest comes for their drink, add ice cubes and then top up each glass with a splash of cold champagne to serve.

The alcohol is cleaner, it's got agave rather than sugar to keep everything on an even keel and you've mixed it all with soft drinks and fresh ingredients into a long drink to help your guests have more staying power. It's like drinking a summer hat. And it all keeps the heat off your head the next day.

Chill-Out Limeade

Here's a recipe that's perfect to offer on a summer's day. It's a touch complex but a wonderfully welcome drink that can all be prepared in advance. If you're having a garden party I'd recommend splashing out on a barman for the evening. They can mix the cocktails properly and effortlessly leaving you free to mingle.

MAKES 8 GLASSES
1 large cucumber, coarsely grated
Juice of ½ lemon
50g bunch of fresh mint, leaves picked, half gently bruised
in a pestle and mortar
100ml elderflower cordial
1 bottle good-quality champagne

With your hands, squeeze the grated cucumber over a fine sieve into
a bowl or jug. Add the lemon juice and the bruised mint leaves and
leave to infuse for one hour. Add the elderflower cordial and chill.
Wrap the remaining mint leaves in damp kitchen paper and chill. Place
eight champagne flutes in the freezer twenty minutes before serving.
Meanwhile, shred the reserved mint leaves. To serve, divide the cordial
mixture among the glasses, then top up with chilled champagne and
garnish with the shredded mint.

SERVING CHAMPAGNE AT PARTIES (SITTING DOWN)

If your guests are seated for a dinner, that's a different matter altogether and feel free to offer champagne by the bottle. All the juggling of glasses is removed, everyone's going to eat and will drink water and there'll be none of that edgey panic as people eye up where their next drink's coming from. It can be an expensive way to go about things, though, so, personally, I'd still say consider saving costs and going for cocktails (following my Positive-Drinking rules) unless it's an intimate dinner party with a small number of guests.

So, what champagne do you serve? Well, that's another Frequently Asked Question.

FAQ: How do I choose champagne?

'I'll stick with gin. Champagne is just ginger ale that knows somebody.'
Hawkeye, M*A*S*H

The amount you spend is no indicator of the size of hangover the drink brings, I'm afraid. I was once offered a champagne that cost £2,000 a bottle and it was so oaky I felt as though I was drinking an old school desk.

A far better plan is to choose your champagne by sugar content. The drier the champagne, the less sugar it will have had added, therefore the less carbs it will have, the less calories and the less negative impact on the body.

The label will tell you the sweetness, and thus the sugar content of the champagne.

Put in increasing order of sugar, the list goes:

1. Ultra or Extra Brut (the driest)
2. Brut
3. Extra Dry

4. Sec

5. Demi-Sec

6. Doux (the sweetest)

Hangover-wise opt for Extra Brut – it is light, crisp, fresh. It's a prima ballerina dancing on your taste buds, whereas Doux is Mrs Doubtfire doing the rumba on your head the next morning.

Laurent Perrier Ultra Brut is an excellent brand to look for. It's sugar-free and is just 60 calories per glass. Or the internationally renowned Wine and Spirits buyer at Harvey Nichols, Ivan Dixon, recommends the Agrapart & Fils Champagne Grand Cru AC 2005 Extra-Brut Mineral, which retails at Harvey Nichols at £39.58, is produced to the highest standards and is entirely free of pesticides or weedkillers.

FAQ: I've got a bottle of champagne, now what do I do with it?

People panic a bit with champagne. How to open it. How to chill it. Here's how.

Firstly. You must serve champagne cold.

Let it go even slightly warm and a lot of them are so dry it'll feel like a leather strap round your neck. The perfect temperature you need is between 43 to 48°F (7°C). The easiest way to achieve this is to plunge an unopened bottle into an ice bucket (half ice and half water). It'll take about twenty minutes.

If you're the sort of person who is always admirably prepared, put it in the fridge, flat on the shelf, for at least three hours before opening.

Experts say you shouldn't ever really put it in the freezer as it can ruin the aroma and flavours, but I say it's forgivable in an emergency. If needs must, stick it in there for no longer than ten minutes and there shouldn't be too much harm done.

Never *ever* put ice in neat champagne. It totally ruins it. Look, it only takes ten minutes to get it ready in the freezer compartment, for goodness' sake. If things are really that desperate you can always pour yourself a Margarita whilst you're waiting.

HOW TO OPEN THE BOTTLE

Men at dinner parties are often handed a bottle, but instead of looking heroic and dealing with it with panache, they often shrink away in terror, worrying they'll make an ass of themselves or take someone's eye out, or that everyone expects them to replicate the winning podium at Formula One and spray it everywhere.

Now those Formula One chaps are very good at driving, but they have absolutely no idea how a bottle should be opened.

This is how to do it:

1. Trying not to shake the bottle at any point, lift it from the ice bucket, dry the bottle with a cloth and then take the foil off the top part around the cork.

2. Hold a cloth over the top of the cork and turn the ring on the wire cage six half-turns to the left so that it's loose.

3. Now we're ready to open it. Point the neck at a 45-degree angle away from you (or any person or object you are fond of), just in case the cork shoots out. Remove the wire cage.

4. Hold the **CORK** still, and then gently turn the **BOTTLE** until the cork slips out.

5. A champagne bottle should open with a sigh. A gentle kiss. **Not an attention-seeking explosion.**

6. Done this way there shouldn't be a drop wasted, but if guests are present it's always best to have a glass nearby in case you mess the whole thing up and the champagne comes gushing out of the bottle and you need to emergency decant with grace.

7. If on your own, of course, you can just gleefully slurp from the fountain of bubbles and pretend to be Michael Schumacher.

8. Serve in flute glasses – those flat seventies-style champagne glasses will ruin all the fizz – and pour an inch into each guest's glass and let it settle, then top up the glasses to about two-thirds full. This stops any frothing over, and stops that awful trick I've seen at dinner parties where people stick their finger in the glass to stop the frothing. This trick does work but it's hardly as elegantly sexy as pouring in the correct manner, which will build a delicious anticipation for the drinkers. Of course, if you're on your own feel free to stick whatever you want in it.

If you can, serve it in crystal flutes. There are all sorts of science books out there that claim it adds to the crispness of the bubbles. Personally I just like them because they do a good solid clink as you raise them for a toast, which always feels wondrously uniting and celebratory.

DRESSING FOR DRINKING

FAQ: Do I really need to follow dress codes for champagne parties? Black tie seems such a major effort.

*'A cause may be inconvenient but it's magnificent.
It's like champagne or high heels and one must be
prepared to suffer for it.'*
Arnold Bennett

Obviously this question doesn't relate only to champagne. But this seems a sensible place to go into some of the sartorial advice that I'll be happy to dispense in my quest to get you Drinking Positively.

WINTER DRINKING

It's fair to meet dress codes if your host has made an effort. For example, if they've paid to put you in a castle for the evening it's only polite to arrive looking exquisite.

So, if the invite specifies cocktail dress, go for a glamorous dress, wear jewellery and high heels. If it's a military occasion then your dress should be full length, however outside a military mess, in current dress codes, a skirt above the knee is perfectly acceptable. Just keep your knees below your waist at all times.

If the invite says 'black tie' or 'evening wear', go for a full-length evening gown. However, there's no need to spend a fortune on a gown for an informal drinks gathering. If it's just a warm white wine round the office photocopier then frankly I wouldn't allow your sartorial bill to go much over the cost of a reasonable bottle of plonk either.

But don't allow yourself to be in discomfort during a party. People often don't think through the elements when they are organising parties. The English are the worst for this as they're fixated with hiring castles for celebrations. It seems a New Year's celebration just simply won't do unless there's a turret or two in sight over the canapés, and then they want everything to look nice in the photographs and go and insist you wear black tie. It's OK for men in tuxedos who can nestle amongst the warming layers of black tie looking both heroic and warm, or dance around in kilts at Scottish balls to keep the blood flowing, but for ladies at black tie events it's a nightmare because ball gowns are desperately cold flimsy things in which to party. Plunging décolletages mean icicles on their chesticles and no stockings are worn in order to keep that delicate Manolo Blahnik shoe on, so bare legs are dangling beneath voluminous skirts. When the wind blows up your skirt it's freezing. It's worse still if you're wearing one of those dresses with a hoop in them to keep the skirts in shape. It's like being in a cathedral, with the wind blowing straight through to the nave.

It's no wonder all the Royals and titled gentry end up in bed with each other. They're just trying to keep warm.

There's a way round the draftiness. Princess Diana gave me the secret to this one too – delicate cashmere long johns. End them at the knee so they'll never be seen, but pop them on so you look effortlessly toasty and regal despite the raging gale straight up your Arc de Triomphe.

When it comes to other dress codes, I'd say don't see them as a pain. Embrace them. Clothing can be used in a cunning manner if you just plan it a bit in advance.

A POSITIVE GUIDE TO HATS

If your champagne invite is for a christening, a wedding or the horse races and hats are called for, then the female guest should choose her headwear with care. Think what you are going to do in your hat and what you wish to happen to you, and choose your hat accordingly. Do you wish to mingle, or stay single?

DISTANCING HATS

If, say, you're forced to go along to a dreadful in-laws' or work colleague's do, a particularly unpleasant child's christening who you really can't bear, or someone's wedding where you wish you'd been the bride, then pick a hat with a really large brim. These are 'distancing

hats' and will ensure you are left alone to enjoy the champagne and the cocktails at the bar in peace. The brim is so large that no one can get close. It will discourage people from speaking to you because you're half person, half hat. You are quite definitely in a world of your own. A little satellite. You can end any conversation simply by lowering your chin and shutting them out so you can just get on with sipping your cocktail. Plus, they look absolutely stunning in photos.

If you really dislike the host, wear a veil too. (In white if you really want to make a point at a wedding and are desperately not keen on the bride that should have been you.)

These big-brimmed distancing hats are also great for warring couples. Any wife in a bad mood with her husband can fend him off with a wide brim and cut him out completely. Likewise, any gentleman who does not wish to talk to his wife or mother-in-law for the event can guarantee himself some peace and quiet by buying her a satellite-sized hat as a surprise gift. It will not only make you look like the good guy who buys superb presents at random, it will also happily prevent her from coming within a foot of your personal space.

In fact, distancing hats are an excellent way of judging the state of a relationship between any couple. When any woman floats in wearing a large-brimmed one, it's a sure-fire indicator she's on the absolute brink of break-up.

THE TACTICAL SEDUCTION HAT

If you have a love target in mind you may wish to go for a 'tactical hat'. This is a hat with a large brim that tilts off to one side. It is extremely useful for fending off love rivals in a group and for enticing the man you have designs on. You can approach the man of your desire with

the hatless side of your head, and whisper sweet nothings in his ear. It's like a little curtain that you can draw.

The hat will prevent anyone else from joining the conversation and completely block his view of anyone else too. If you're conducting secret conversations or illicit affairs it also enables you to effortlessly block off any curious onlookers.

Of course, if any woman wearing a tilted hat starts approaching your man you should know what that scurrilous minx has planned. If a seductress in a tactical hat is seated at your table for dinner, I'd advise that you pop in there early and check the seating plan, and swap the place cards around so he's sitting to her hat side to block her off from the start.

Of course, these hats are also amazingly effective for escaping from dull dinner companions. If anyone's insisting on boring you to death you can always tilt your hat to their side to block the bores out.

In emergencies, where you know you will be bored by both sides, or really don't feel like talking to anyone, you can always go for an ear-covering Jane Eyre style bonnet. If anyone asks why you're wearing it, blame Vivienne Westwood and tell them it's all the rage in fashionable circles.

SOCIABLE HATS FOR SINGLETON LADIES

If you arrive at any drinking event alone and don't wish to leave that way then, ladies, go for a small brim. And put your hair up. I see girls with hair hanging lankily about under hats out at the polo or weddings, standing about hopefully. Sadly, I know they're in for a disappointing evening. Anyone approaching them will have to wade through acres of stringy hair before they get anywhere near their ears to whisper something nice.

With the hair drawn up neatly under a hat, you can bob and weave and dance and laugh and not a hair will go out of place. You'll permanently offer a coquettish ear for gossip and remain in proper trim and always ready to be adored.

Personally, when hat codes are given and I'm feeling sociable I think a well-chosen fascinator is always a delight. It's usually perfectly acceptable in place of a hat. I have one headpiece that can adapt to all occasions so I can make a decision when I get there depending on the company – it consists of two of my pet parrot Max's tail feathers arranged over some diamonds. On good days his tail feathers point straight up and anyone can approach my ears. But if it turns out the party's crammed with less than thrilling and entertaining company, I simply set it at a right angle to my head and I can ward off all dullards and unwanted cocktail companions to a radius of two feet.

A POSITIVE GUIDE TO CORSETS AND TIGHT BELTS

Never drink too much champagne whilst wearing a tight corset, or too tightly belted trousers. The bubbles all come back up and make you hiccup. Or bloat. Or worse, have a jet-propulsion incident like Hovercraft Hetty. Always ensure a loose or flexible waistband for maximum enjoyment.

'A woman should never be seen eating or drinking, unless it be lobster salad and champagne, the only true feminine and becoming viands.'
Lord Byron

'Frankly, with his reputation, I'd recommend you put on a distancing hat and don't get taken in by the hype.'
Cleo Rocos

Just to check you've been paying attention, here's one of my little quizzes again.

HOW WELL ARE YOU DOING?

THE POSITIVE DRINKING CHAMPAGNE QUIZ

How much champagne should you drink when at an incredibly important summer party hosted by the boss?

☐ None Oh come on. Look, I said champagne could be evil like a supermodel but at least put your toe on the red carpet and join in. Have a sip, come on. One glass helps you to relax and prolong your fabulousness for the duration of the party.

☐ Two glasses Well done. Like diamond earrings, two is an ideal, chic amount.

☐ A Bottle OK. So that's about six glasses. You know, things probably started to deteriorate after three. But listen. This is completely understandable. Don't do yourself down. It was the glass of aspirations that led you astray. Have a large glass of water and I hope that giant hippos don't trip the light fantastic on your head in the morning.

☐ A Magnum (2 bottles) Ah. Yes. There are photos. Good time, was it? Did you get confused when someone asked if you'd 'like another one'? Just for clarity. They meant a glass, not a bottle. Still, it's not your fault. It's that damned champagne glass, isn't it? You didn't want to put it down. I'd advise you to find someone who was worse than you, track down some photographic evidence and distribute it round the office email immediately.

☐ A Nebuchadnezzer (20 bottles) Or what felt like it at least. You lost count after three. Did you wake up hanging onto the shag-pile carpet praying the world would stop this morning? Perhaps you need to check out the Prehab chapter on page 197 . . .

What hat should you wear to the mother-in-law's drinks party?

☐ A balaclava Hmmm. A touch antisocial. Still, it'll stop her criticizing your hair.

☐ A tin helmet Hmmmm. Again. Maybe a little too obvious you hate the old battle axe.

☐ A tilted distancing hat Perfect. You can proffer a cheek for an icy greeting, then simply stand next to her, hat side facing her, and she shouldn't disturb you again.

☐ An eighteenth-century reinforced bonnet with built-in sound system. Ah. You don't get on, I take it?

'Too much of anything is bad, but too much champagne is just right.'
Mark Twain

'In victory, you deserve champagne, in defeat, you need it.'
Napoleon Bonaparte

RIGHT. THAT'S CHAMPAGNE COVERED THEN.
CAN I TEMPT ANYONE TO A GLASS OF WINE?

LESSON FIVE

HOW NOT TO WHINE ABOUT WINE

(INCLUDING STAIN-REMOVAL TIPS)

'Wine is a turncoat; first a friend and then an enemy.'
Henry Fielding

*'And red wine can all too often strike your sofa.
Let me tell you how to get it out.'*
Cleo Rocos

Look, we could stay here all day talking about wine. Talking about the ins and outs of 'grapes', 'legs' and 'vintages'. But life, and lunchtimes, are just too short.

Personally, I have found the following two pieces of advice get me through every occasion. They were given to me by a Maître d' at a Michelin-starred restaurant. Basically this is all you really need:

1. If buying from a supermarket, spend over a tenner on a bottle and it should work out fine. OK, so that's not cheap, but it'll mean you're a little more careful about drinking it, and you'll be drinking something a little more 'considered'.

2.   If being served wine in a restaurant and you want to impress, then savour it slowly and pronounce that it is: 'very indicative of the region'. If it's red, you can then, after a further few seconds contemplation, announce: 'It's jammy, isn't it?' This will impress most people. The Maître d' confessed it's all he says as he's handing over a £200 bottle of wine to someone and they always seem quite happy.

Now, of course, there will be occasions when you're in trouble and a ten-pound bottle to say sorry simply will not do. With that in mind, here is my guide to buying expensive wine. Choose your wine to your crime:

I'm in minor trouble with my spouse/boss/I need to thank someone for looking after my pet. Look for something with AOC on the front, which stands for Apellation d'origine Contrôlée and guarantees it's a decent French wine made to a high standard. Spend just over a tenner and it will be fine.

I'm in medium-level trouble with the spouse/boss/I'm really sorry about what my pet did to the sofa of the person who was looking after it. Hmmm, maybe something with Premier Cru or 'first growth' written on the front is needed. Expect to pay about £20 to see you through this one.

I have done major damage to the spouse's car/I've done something in front of the boss at his dinner party that will involve a dry cleaning

bill/I'm terribly sorry, I've lost/killed your pet In that case, I'd say you'd better go for something with Grand Cru on the front. Don't expect to get much change out of £100.

I know exactly who can help with the best tips on this one, my good friend and renowned wine expert Kyri Sotiri, director of Soho Wine Supply Ltd.

POSSIBLE WINE HEADACHE TRIGGERS

If you suffer dreadfully from red wine headaches, or suffer from allergic symptoms from drinking it, then it may be down to the various naturally occurring compounds in red wine.

A little label research can go a long way to helping you here as it is most likely that your symptoms are being triggered by sulphites, tannins, histamines, or tyramines. Let's go through this list of suspects, what they do and how to avoid their ill effects.

Allergy or Asthma symptoms

Sulphites occur naturally during the fermentation process, but in addition to this, Sulphur Dioxide (SO_2) is usually added in small quantities to prevent the growth of unwanted bacteria and to stabilize and preserve wine. When used sparingly, this compound is an important component of healthy wine, and wines that have been produced without any added SO_2 are notoriously unstable.

However, medical research has shown that sulphites may cause allergy and asthma symptoms in certain people. So search for low-sulphite wines if you find wine triggers these symptoms. Even if the wine is labelled 'EU organic', it can still contain high sulphite levels so check it is specifically labelled 'low sulphite' or 'sulphite free'. A lovely example to search for are the wines from the family winery Domaine Viret. Do be aware that wine that is sulphite free will be more unstable so it's best consumed on the day of opening. So tell your guests to finish the bottle for chemical reasons, and have both a clear head and a clear conscience the next day.

Headaches or Migraines

Tannins are complex compounds derived from the skin, stems and seeds of the grape. Simply put, tannins give colour to red wine whilst also being responsible for imparting structure and a 'mouth-puckering' quality.

Studies have shown that tannins cause the release of serotonin, which at high levels can lead to headaches and, in a certain percentage of the population, migraines.

So, if you feel that you may be sensitive to tannin but you wish to drink red wine, try examples made with the grapes Pinot Noir, Gamay and Sangiovese. I list some lovely examples on p 74.

If this doesn't rule it out, you may find that you are sensitive to histamines or Tyramine.

Histamines can be found to be up to 200 per cent higher in red wine than in white. Those who are sensitive to them lack a particular enzyme in their intestines that can help them metabolize histamines, and it is believed that the combination of alcohol and this deficiency can cause them headaches. Switch to white wines and see if this helps.

Tyramine is known for causing the tightening of blood vessels and increasing blood pressure, which again triggers headaches in some people. These same people might get headaches from aged cheeses, smoked or cured meats, and citrus fruit.

Again, white wine may be the way forward for you as white wine is generally far less likely to trigger headaches, especially migraines, as the juice is usually fermented away from the grape skins.

Organic and Biodynamic Wine

If you suffer from hangovers on red wine, try a bottle of biodynamic wine. The results can be quite phenomenal, leaving you fresh and clear headed after even quite a long session.

Both organic and biodynamic producers use sound winemaking and agricultural principles when producing their wine. Given that there are up to 200 approved chemicals/additives that can be legally added to wine, this gives you a guaranteed cleaner drink. They are similar in the sense that they do not use any artificial chemicals, but biodynamic goes further.

Actually, some of it does sound rather on the eccentric side and involves burying cow horns full of manure to channel new life into the soil, but the result is an incredibly high quality wine, which is free of preservatives and really does help the head the next day. And even if critics knock all the mysticism around it, there's no denying that the end result is a high quality wine.

Biodynamic needn't be massively expensive either. Gran Cerdo, (Spanish for Big Pig) is a biodynamic, natural Rioja with minimal sulphur, which (at the time of printing) comes in at under £9. Look out for the jolly picture of a pig on the front and entertaining rant about bankers on the label at the back. Its maker, the magnificently named Gonzalo Gonzalo Grijalba is renowned as an eco warrior, who was inspired to develop natural treatments for vineyards after witnessing his winemaker father become ill after years of exposure to the chemicals used in vineyards.

It should be noted, however, that biodynamic is not the only way forward, there are many fine wine producers who are not certified organic or biodynamic and who are diligent in their vineyard and winemaking practices, producing some simply stunning wine.

Leading wine retailers have compiled this little list of wonders for you to look out for on your travels, which could help you avoid the headache triggers listed above. They are both excellent value and well made:

Red:
    Fleurie 'La Madone' – Vintage 2009
    Albert Bichot (£10.99)
      Beaujolais, France
    · (100 per cent Gamay)

    Chianti Classico – Vintage 2006
    Il Molino di Grace (£16.50)
      Tuscany, Italy
      (100 per cent Sangiovese)

    Estate Pinot Noir – Vintage 2007
    Pirie (£17.00)
      Tamar Valley, Tasmania
      (100 per cent Pinot Noir)

Jones Block Shiraz – Vintage 2005
Paxton (£25.50)
  McClaren Vale, Australia
  (Biodynamic – 100 per cent Shiraz)

White:
  Picpoul de Pinet – Vintage 2010
  Mas de Mas (£10.00)
    Languedoc-Roussillon, France
    (100 per cent Picpoul)

  Adoro Sauvignon Blanc – Vintage 2008
  Adoro (£14.50)
    Multi-regional, South Africa
    (100 per cent Sauvignon Blanc)

  Steingarten Riesling – Vintage 2007
  Jacob's Creek (£15.95)
    Barossa Valley, Australia
    (100 per cent Riesling)

  Chablis Premier Cru 'Les Vaillons' – Vintage 2010
  Domaine Long Depaquit (£18.95)
    Chablis, France
    (100 per cent Chardonnay)

Of course, all this is fabulous advice if you're at home and you've bought the wine. But things get trickier if you're out at a party and at the mercy of another buyer.

'Age is just a number. It's totally irrelevant unless, of course, you happen to be a bottle of wine.'
Joan Collins

WINE AT PARTIES

There is one golden rule at parties:

Never. Ever. Drink the Wine Punch.

No good has ever come of this. You have no idea what is in it.

Personally, I'd avoid all wine like the plague at parties. Unless your host is really into wine, wealthy and has good taste, you never quite know what you're getting. If you can't see the bottle and the wine has been pre-poured then I'd assume the worst because that's probably what you're being served.

White wine, when served chilled (remember, I can't say it often enough, always be wary of the quality of any drink that MUST be served CHILLED), can make even the most hideous stuff become palatable and it's not until you wake up the next morning feeling that your head is five times larger than your body that you realise the damage you've done.

If you have to drink wine at a party then, for goodness' sake, drink water. Lots of it. It's the only thing that's going to save you.

Of course, the problem with water is that it means repeated trips to the facilities. Don't worry. Let me deal with that one. Let me tell you about 'The Investment Wee'. It was a member of a royal family who imparted me with this miraculous piece of advice on how to drink lots of water without having repeated trips to the throne room. I shall forever remain indebted to her.

THE INVESTMENT WEE

It was a question I'd always pondered about the Royals and the A-listers – with all eyes on them for each event, how on earth do they avoid going to the lavatory? You never see a Hollywood star in the queue for the loo, do you? And there's never been a recorded case where a Royal has been called up to do the speeches at a Do and everyone's had to hang on for a few minutes and await the Royal flush.

There's a trick that they're all taught apparently. Let me try to describe it as delicately as I can.

Have you noticed that the first time you ever 'go' at a drinks party, you can hold off for hours, but after that, when you give in and visit the smallest room, you have to keep giving in? You end up repeatedly scurrying for relief like a puppy, constantly having to excuse yourself from jolly conversations to go again and again?

To avoid this, before any event go to the smallest room and do what you have to do. Then sit tight. And wait there for a minute. And go again. Even when you feel you have no more to give you will find there is a small amount that acts like a frequent trigger if you do not expel it from your bladder. It sets you up. Trains things. It will dramatically increase the amount of time you have before you need to go again. Do try it. It works. And leaves more time for adventures and meeting fabulous people.

*'You're not drunk if you can lie on the floor
without holding on.'*
Dean Martin

YOUR OWN PARTY

At your own party buy the best wine you can afford. It's the most polite thing to do for your guests. You owe it to them not to let them get hung-over. It doesn't all have to be Grand Cru, but do try to steer away from anything served in a box. And always make sure you buy enough – many wine-sellers will supply cases on a sale-or-return basis, in the unlikely event you have any left over. You don't want to be stuck serving whatever the guests have brought: it may mix horribly with what you chose to serve them, and it's a Russian Roulette working out whether they have brought you something divine for you to enjoy when all the thirsty guests are out of the way, or something appallingly cut-throat they found stuck down the back of their wine rack or from the corner shop on the way.

FAQ: How do I remove red wine stains?

If you serve red wine, trust me. It will, nine times out of ten, be spilt by someone. Some of it will end up on your floor. Some of it will end up on the walls. Some of it will end up on various small pets, children, in-laws and furnishings. This is a part of life. Let's deal with it.

REMOVING RED WINE STAINS

The first rule of red wine stains is don't despair. Stains are all part of a good night out or in. They're souvenirs. Don't be too precious.

Don't demand everyone remove their shoes as they walk in and sit there awkwardly. Unless for religious purposes, I always find that quite rude. My shoes are part of my outfit. I want to wear them. Floors are for walking on. If people want to dance on the table, let them. If they want to waltz around with their wine in their hands, let them. It's a glorious party!

I dislike evenings where you sit there on pristine furniture and everyone feels as though they're wrapped in cling-film. I much prefer to go to a house where everyone feels like they can just kick back and enjoy themselves. If you're going to entertain, entertain.

I have a beautiful large antique rug that I throw on the floor for parties. If wine gets dropped on it, wine gets dropped on it. It kind of adds to the pattern. I only ever buy sofas with removable and washable covers and if you or your guests are red wine fiends I suggest you do the same. If anything is spilled throw some carbonated or soda water over it as an immediate measure and throw it in the wash. White wine is also famous for neutralising the staining power of red wine: without wasting too much of your precious blanco, a splash of white over the offending red will take the sting out of the stain once you're ready to wash the item properly.

Sofas/Dining chairs

If you have dry-clean-only furniture you're a fool to yourself and I suggest you invest in a few stylish throws. But, aside from that – have this dry-clean solution mixed up ready in a cupboard for emergency red wine stain removal: mix together one part water, one part isopropyl rubbing alcohol 90%, and one part white vinegar.

(I don't have to tell you not to drink this, do I? It's not a cocktail, OK?)

Apply a small amount to the stain, pat with a sponge, and then, using a vacuum-cleaner pipe, vacuum the stain and all around it, which should prevent a water mark. Test a small patch first, although frankly if you've got a whacking great red wine stain in the middle of the thing it will be hard to make it worse.

This method also works on beer, cocktails, liqueurs, and, if it's really been a wild night, mustard.

Don't ask me how I know this but if it's been a really lively night and you've got candlewax stains on the furnishings too then an excellent trick is to put a cloth over the top, put your iron on its lowest possible setting and iron over the top of the spilled wax and it will come out. Note I said the lowest setting. Anything higher and you'll end up with scorch marks. Trying to explain away a scorch mark, candlewax and a red wine stain on the sofa can be a little tricky.

Walls

Having seen how successfully someone I know has deployed this remedy, the first thing I put in my trolley when planning to serve red wine at my party at home, is paint. The best hosts I know have spare sample-sized pots of all their home wall paints. I had dinner with a divine TV doctor, who watched calmly as an entire bottle of Burgundy was sent accidentally smashing against a wall. Instead of reaching for a cloth in a panic, he calmly waited for it all to dry then simply repainted the walls the next morning.

Your face

The problem with red wine is that it does turn you a bit vampirical after a couple of glasses. If you're drinking it on a first date and your date is not, then do take a toothbrush with you to have a quick brush-up at the end of the meal prior to any kissing. And try to eat in a half-light. Those red-stained lips will not be alluring in a full beam. I therefore recommend a good white wine or Skinny Tequila cocktail for a first date.

With red wine, the morning after, when you greet your reflection in the mirror to find you have a red-rimmed stain on your lips, just brush them with an electric toothbrush. The stains will vanish from your lips. If your face feels somewhat leathery after a night on the old rouge then using a [different] toothbrush head, simply lightly brush your face. I know it all sounds a little odd, but I gleaned this tip from a dermatologist and it's just the thing for pepping and brightening up your complexion and getting the blood circulating again.

I'd probably avoid doing this in front of anyone else. No matter how sensational you were last night, the sight of you enthusiastically brushing your entire face with their Oral B may prove a bit much for some people.

Wine Hangover Avoidance

As a final tip on wine, if you are intending to drink a lot in an evening and you are not sure of the quality you're having, try to only ever drink it with people you like. Always try to drink wine in situations where you are going to be laughing and dancing instead of letting yourself slide into a sugary slump of emotional turmoil.

The reason why is my breathing theory. It was taught to me by a Californian road cop.

Breathing Theory

Have you ever noticed that if you spend an evening with someone dull and judgemental you'll feel like death the next day, yet you can spent the most deliciously decadent night out with happy, enchanting people and wake up bright and breezy? The morning after the headstand competition with Mr Nicholson I fully deserved to have a monumental hangover as I went way over the two-Martini recommended levels. But we all laughed and tangoed throughout the night and I was more than deliciously fine.

The science behind it is lots of breathing.

The rather chatty Californian traffic cop who told me this worked in the breathalyser department stopping people on the highways and measuring how far over the limit they were.

As he explained, those breathalyser things work out how much alcohol there is in your body by working out how much is in your breath when you breathe out. So the more you breathe out, the less alcohol there is in your body. It's only logical, isn't it?

I could go into some more scientific thing here about how alcohol is broken down and shifted about in the body and finds its way into the lungs, but life is too short or is that too long? Just trust me. If you laugh more, dance more and party more on a night out, you'll breathe out more and your hangover won't be as bad.

If you sit there, bored stiff, you'll breathe less. So don't, under any circumstances, drink with dreary people. It truly is bad for your health.

FAQ: But I always seem to get stuck with the office bore at a party. How do I avoid them?

'Fan the sinking flame of hilarity with the wing of friendship; and pass the rosy wine.'
Charles Dickens

OK, so this isn't just a wine question. But believe me, if you're talking about an office party then the wine is bound to be bad. So the last thing you want is to get stuck with someone boring, too.

The first thing I do when entering a party is look and see where most people are laughing and then I head there straight away. If a dull person corners you at a party just simply get out of there. Feign deafness, death, litigation, anything you have to do. Move away. Don't do that terribly polite thing of being dragged into their drearyness for an evening because you fear offending them. These people are usually remarkably thick skinned otherwise they would have learned that it is basic good manners to be entertaining company. Guests should always arrive at a party with at least three amusing or entertaining stories to share. It is extremely rude and totally inexcusable to be dull. If you are not laughing tell yourself you must leave on medical grounds.

An excellent trick I often do to get out of a dull conversation is to pretend that I have suddenly lost a ring or an earring and need to 'retrace my steps' back to the door. You can then pretend to spot it glistening on the floor near the 'interesting' group of people and happily deposit yourself over there as you allegedly find it. I once actually became so desperately bored with a dreary diplomat, that

I started making dramatic hand gestures to explain a joke, ending with a grand finale of hand flinging that happily enabled me to send my large ring flying right across a dance floor and hurtling towards a gathering of rather handsome Olympic medalists.

I don't drink with bores. People who tut, count units and stare disapprovingly at your glass, people who get in work mode and never step out of it. These are the people who contribute greatly to giving you hangovers.

So never be embarrassed to show an absolutely gleefully silly side of yourself after a cocktail. The best people do this. I promise. I fondly remember a dinner watching the Chief Justice of Nigeria singing 'Summertime' standing on the table at a dinner party in Motcombs restaurant in Belgravia. And elsewhere in this book I'll tell you of a quite stupendous night getting out of breath through a high-kicking contest with Gore Vidal. Both of them fabulous men who I bet rarely had a hangover because they laughed so joyously on their nights off.

FAQ: I was given a bottle of cheap wine by a neighbour. I'm never looking after their stupid pet again, I can tell you, but meanwhile, is there anything I can do with it?

'I cook with wine, sometimes I even add it to the food.'
W. C. Fields

If you're given a bottle of sub-standard wine as a present, or have a few lesser quality bottles left over from a dinner party, don't despair.

Divide them into ice-cube trays and freeze, and, when making gravy in the future, add a couple of shots to cheer things up. So, sorry the neighbour was such a tightwad, but at least you may get a half-decent dinner out of it.

'Wino Forever'

Johnny Depp's tattoo (Which once read 'Winona Forever')

LESSON SIX

HOW TO TUCK INTO TEQUILA

'One tequila, two tequila, three tequila, floor.'
George Carlin

'Dear Mr Carlin, you should have read my guidance on 100 per cent agave tequila. Drink what I tell you and you'll be perfectly fine.'
Cleo Rocos

They say money can't buy you happiness. Well, I say that those people simply aren't buying the right tequila.

I love tequila. It is my absolute favourite drink – a subject close to my heart, and even closer to my drinks cabinet. In fact, I am something of a tequila evangelist and that has not gone unnoticed by the Mexican government and the major tequila producers. In 2009 I was invited by the President of the tequila industry and my dear friend Tomas Estes, tequila ambassador to Europe, to attend their high-profile annual meeting in Guadalajara where I was honoured with an award for my dedication to and promotion of the tequila catergory. I am now officially recognised as the Tequila Queen.

Tequila is made from the agave plant, a plant ripened between six and eight years in beautiful mineral-rich volcanic soil in Mexican sun. This is a plant that has had a truly fabulous life. And, once distilled into a glass, I like to think of it as the plant that will unashamedly nourish you with good and glorious times.

Now, all of this passion for this wonderful drink started from a sunny day in Mexico around nine years ago when I spotted an elegant, beautiful lady in her sixties, sitting at a table, writing, and sipping from a blue fluted glass. She looked like a *Vogue* cover. Radiating elegance. With just a little edge of danger in her glass.

I had to ask what she was drinking. The answer was tequila. Served the way they do in Mexico. Straight. Room temperature. In a little glass. And sipped.

Now, I hated tequila. Or at least I thought I did. I'd only ever had it accompanied by a shuddering mix of lime and salt and thrown back in a shot glass. But I bought it this day and I drank it the way they do in Mexico. This was my first 100 per cent agave tequila. This is why it tasted and felt so different to drink. I sipped it, I loved it and I never, ever looked back.

If you mix and serve tequila following the rules I describe below, it is an absolute tonic of a drink, which delivers radiating happiness in a glass. You just feel great.

You can serve tequila straight, or in a cocktail. But there are three rules to drinking tequila:

Only drink 100 per cent agave tequila.

Only ever mix it with pure, natural ingredients.

Only drink tequila. Sip don't Shoot and Do Not Mix with Other Alcohols.

There are two categories of tequila:

Tequila (mix or blended).

Mixed tequilas are made using a minimum of 51 per cent Blue Weber agave mixed with sugarcane or corn sugar alcohols.

100 per cent agave tequila.

The 100 per cent agave tequilas are made only from the Blue Weber agave plant.

FAQ: Hang on. Every time I've drunk tequila I've ended up with a horrendous headache. Are you seriously telling me you can drink tequila without getting a hangover?

Yes you can. But if, and ONLY if, you follow
the first rule of tequila.

Only drink 100 per cent agave tequila

The first thing you must look for on the tequila bottle are the words '100 per cent agave'. If it doesn't say this on the bottle do not go near it. Or at least do not embark on an evening drinking it and think that you had a real tequila and certainly don't expect to come out the other end unscathed.

This label marking – 100 per cent agave – has nothing to do with strength. It is a mark of purity. It means it is made only from the Blue Weber agave plant. It has been produced by a system that is the most strictly regulated in the world and is the purest form of the drink you can buy. If you drink this, and only this, **you won't have a hangover.**

FAQ: So this is going to be expensive then? Or only available from specialist shops?

Not at all. 100 per cent agave does not necessarily mean it is more expensive than mixed (51 per cent agave) brands. There are numerous good quality 100 per cent agave tequila brands on the market for under £25, including my own premium award winning brand AquaRiva Reposado Tequila which is readily available in Waitrose and Sainsburys. At twenty-seven shots in a bottle, that works out at under £1 per drink.

The second rule of tequila is:
only ever mix it with pure, natural ingredients

Do NOT buy those ready-made mixers in shops. They are laden with sugar as well as other unhealthy ingredients. It's really easy and cheap to buy fresh limes and organic agave syrup and to mix them yourself and I'll give you all the recipes you need in a little while. Tequila is a lovely clean drink, keep it that way with fresh fruits and ingredients. Get rid of the sugar, maximise the taste and eliminate the hangover.

The third rule of tequila is:
only drink tequila. Sip Don't Shoot
and Do Not Mix with Other Alcohols

Well, you can get away with a tiny fresh splash of champagne in a cocktail. But the trick is to avoid mixing in a few red wines after a night on tequila, or having tequila cocktails that contain other liquors. As a basic rule of thumb, you should especially avoid the cocktails that mix tequila with sticky alcohols such as Cointreau or triple sec etc. This is not a good combination. It's a headache in a glass.

And never start with tequila cocktails and segue into brandies and Armagnacs after dinner. Instead, go for brandy-like flavours of tequila – the Anejos or Extra Anejos which I describe below. These tequilas are exquisite and complex. Great brandy- whisky- and Cognac-lovers are often converted. Sipping Anejo after an evening of tequila/ tequila cocktails gives all the taste but stops any mixing of alcohols and therefore any hangover.

FAQ: So, help me through the minefield. What's the difference between all the different sorts of tequila?

FLAVOURS OF TEQUILA

There are as many tequila tastes out there as whiskeys and wines. They range from fiery to delicate citrus with almond flavour to a more oaky whisky or cognac flavour. Let me go through the different types.

Blanco/Plata/Silver: The Blanco is the youngest, un-aged and colourless, it is the baby of the category with a more noticeable and fuller agave flavour, often a little fiery. Serve it in a cocktail and it will bring a summery kick of happiness. Serve it straight and it's a wonderful accompaniment to spicy food and like all pure tequilas, wonderfully gentle on the stomach.

Reposado: This means rested. Golden in colour, it is aged for between three months and one year in oak barrels. Depending on what it's aged in – such as French oak, new oak barrels or used American bourbon barrels – Reposado takes on a much more complex flavour. American oaks tend to deliver a vanilla like taste, French oaks a more chocolatey taste. It's a little gentler than a Blanco and wonderful straight or in cocktails.

Anejo: This means the old one, and is aged for one to three years. Drink it straight and sip. Again, it's a wonderful end-of-the-evening drink, with all the complexity of a fine whisky or cognac. Experiment with brands. They are brandy-like and flavours range from chocolatey smooth to warm and surrendery.

Worms and other bugs. They are just a marketing gimmick. Never drink anything with a dead animal in it. No matter what the friendly local tells you.

Sample and enjoy them all. Blanco is a tempestuous young movie starlet of a drink on your palate, Reposado a refined and smooth operator. Anejo is a poet rich with verse, Extra Anejo is quite simply the gentle, wise king.

Fancy a night with one of them? Here are some excellent 100 per cent agave tequilas for you to start with, followed by some great recipes:

AquaRiva	El Tesoro
Ocho	Casa Noble
Siete Leguas	Alma Mia

All available online at www.sohowine.co.uk
and www.thedrinkshop.com.

POSITIVE DRINKING TEQUILA PRESCRIPTIONS

The following will leave you hangover-free. If you prepare it exactly how I say and follow the Tequila Rules.

SKINNY HOT TODDY

35ml 100 per cent agave blanco tequila
20ml fresh lime juice
20ml AquaRiva organic agave syrup

Combine the ingredients in a long glass or mug with hot water, garnish with cinnamon stick.

NO-HANGOVER WATERMELON MARGARITA

35ml 100 per cent agave blanco or Reposado tequila
15ml organic agave syrup
25ml fresh lime juice
20ml watermelon juice

Muddle the flesh of a watermelon and strain. Add 20ml of the watermelon juice to the tequila, lime and agave syrup. Shake well and serve in a tall glass. Garnish with watermelon wedge.

TEQUILA COSMOPOLITAN

35ml 100 per cent agave blanco tequila
15ml organic agave syrup
25ml fresh lime juice
6 muddled and strained raspberries

Serve in chilled cocktail glass with fresh fruit garnish.

NO HANGOVER TEQUILA MOJITO

35ml 100 per cent agave Reposado or Anejo tequila
20ml organic agave syrup
25ml fresh lime juice
Fresh mint

Muddle several sprigs of fresh mint in the bottom of a tall glass.
Add all the other ingredients and top up with good-quality club soda.

NO HANGOVER POMEGRANATE MARTINI

35ml 100 per cent agave blanco tequila
15ml organic agave syrup
20ml fresh lime juice or juice of one lime
20ml pomegranate juice

Shake with plenty of ice, strain and serve in a chilled cocktail glass.

NO HANGOVER GUAVARITA

35ml 100 per cent agave AquaRiva tequila blanco or Reposado
25ml fresh lime juice
15ml guava purée or 25ml guava juice
15ml organic agave syrup

Shake with lots of ice, strain into a chilled cocktail glass,
or serve in a rocks glass with ice just like a margarita.

AQUARIVA MAI TAI

20ml AquaRiva Reposado
20ml Alma Mia Reposado
10ml Ocho tequila
3–4 drops of Angustora bitters
10ml AquaRiva organic agave syrup
30ml fresh lime juice
10ml Orgeat syrup

Place all the ingredients into a shaker with ice. Fill a rocks glass with ice
cubes. Shake the cocktail shaker, then strain into the rocks glass and
garnish with lime and mint and stir.

MEXICAN 55

35ml 100 per cent agave blanco or Reposado tequila
15ml fresh lemon juice
15ml organic agave syrup
2 dashes of grapefruit bitters
Champagne or Prosecco

Combine all the ingredients except the champagne then top up with
champagne or prosecco. Serve in a champagne flute.

**FAQ: Seriously. All these cocktails will not give me a
hangover? Even if I drink loads of them?**

Oh yes. I've tested this mix very thoroughly on the most fabulous
people. Why not take the tequila challenge yourself?

*'I've been to the annual dinner of Cleo Rocos' Tequila Society
and tested the assurance that large amounts of pure 100 per
cent agave tequila don't induce a hangover. 'Tis true. Pure
agave tequila leaves you as fresh and bright as the dew on a
morning daisy-button. Plus it's actually very nice. But it has
to be 100 per cent pure agave. Otherwise it tastes like bum
and leaves you wanting to die.'*
Derren Brown

'It doesn't give you a hangover. It's like some sort of wizard's medicine that makes you feel all happy but you're not sick the next day.'

Keith Lemon, the morning after an eleven-hour flight from London to Mexico in which we and our merry bunch of travellers drained the aeroplane dry of all the 100 per cent agave AquaRiva tequila stocked on board.

Richard Branson was so impressed by the hangover-free partying that he took a case to Necker so he could carry on over there.

For more advice about drinking on planes see page 164.

Meanwhile. Anyone fancy a gin?

LESSON SEVEN

HOW TO WIN WITH GIN

'The principal sin, Of Gin, Is, among others,
Ruining mothers.'
ANON

'A touch harsh on what can actually be a very
refreshing drink. Let's see if we can do something
about gin's bad reputation.'
Cleo Rocos

Mother's ruin. Gin-crazed. A gin-soaked drunk. Gin is a spirit that gets a really bad rap. This is all somewhat unfair as all the bad stuff associated with it happened a good two hundred years ago. Personally I always make a point of forgiving any bad behaviour involving alcohol on a much shorter-termer basis.

On the subject of which, here's a hostess tip which works well for me.

FORGIVING DRUNKEN BEHAVIOUR

If you have ever been present at a social event in which someone has over-imbibed, failed to drink positively and embarrassed themselves, then bear in mind that the next time you see them they may well be crippled with embarrassment. Simply defuse the situation by offering them a drink, then feigning bewilderment when they order alcohol and saying: 'Really? Oh darling. I always thought you were teetotal.' You should then never, ever mention their over-indulgence again. If they bring it up, tell them they were fun and charming company and you simply don't remember any bad behaviour. Then maybe lend them this book.

Anyway, back to gin, which has been known to cause party-goers a few nights of bad behaviour. But there are much worse and far more harmful things out there to drink. Select the right brand and serve it properly and gin can actually be one of the most refreshing alcoholic drinks around.

FAQ: So. What is gin?

Gin is essentially a pimped-up vodka – a colourless, flavourless, odourless alcohol with flavours added from herbs and spices known as botanicals. Its main flavouring comes from juniper berries, which give it its name – 'gin' comes from 'Geneva' – the Dutch word for juniper berries.

JUNIPERS

The junipers give gin an instant health benefit – the berries aid water retention and boost kidney function, so if you're ever plagued with bloating try a little gin at night and you can wake up flatter of stomach in the morning. As well as the junipers, some gins contain dozens of different herbs and spices, which I go through on page 104, so you may even absorb the health benefits from all of those too.

ABVS – A QUICK LESSON

The problem with gin is that it's so strong. In order to hold flavourings it needs a higher alcohol by volume (ABV) than some other spirits. As a rough guide, the minimum you're looking at in a decent gin to hold its taste is 40 per cent ABV, but there are brands out there coming in at a gusset-busting, brain-throbbing, tongue numbing 60 per cent ABV. So basically, you really don't want to be drinking this stuff neat. As I remarked earlier, I try to avoid drinking anything over 40 per cent ABV. However, higher ABVs doesn't mean it can't be a positive drink. Mix it up in the ways I describe on page 109, serve it long, and you can bring that high ABV down without losing any of the exquisite flavour the makers have worked so hard to create.

EXPORT – A LESSON FOR UK DRINKERS

Ever wondered why that heavenly cocktail you were sold abroad becomes an insipid and disappointing dinner party cocktail at home?

It's not just about the surroundings and the sunshine, it's all down to the ABVs. Here in the UK we are particularly unlucky with some major brands as they are sold as versions that are as much as 10 per cent ABV weaker than those sold abroad, becoming meek, tasteless versions of the originals. Once the ABV sinks into the thirties then it may be a less powerful drink, but it's very dull, and gin-wise frankly I wouldn't bother – although it still works as an excellent jewellery cleaner (See page 121). So, to avoid disappointment, if you find a brand you like the taste of when abroad, then either stash a bottle in your suitcase when you come back from holiday or look instead for the export versions, which are higher ABV, and then mix it as I prescribe.

IT'S A DIET. HONESTLY

The great news about gin is that it's also an excellent choice if you're looking to shift a little excess poundage. Pick your mixers well and it can be low sugar, and low calorie. Tips on low-calorie tonics, if you missed them, are back on pg 23.

> **FAQ: OK, so if this is practically a medicine, how is it that gin has such a bad reputation?**

Ah, well, as with all things alcoholic, it's about buying the right products and brands. I'm going to tell you a little tale from history about drinking gin. It happened in the seventeenth century, so no I wasn't there. But a desperately poor young mother called Judith Defoe was . . .

THE FALL OF JUDITH DEFOE
A Cautionary Tale About Gin

Seventeenth-century London was awash with cheap, illegal, often lethal forms of gin in the slums. Having started life as a Dutch medicine to treat stomach ailments, the juniper-flavoured liquor arrived in the UK via soldiers campaigning in the Dutch Republic who had tried the so-called 'Dutch Courage' liquor and loved its warming effects. The succession of the Dutchman William of Orange to the British throne in 1688 helped cement things, as he loved this spirit so much he'd hand out drinks licenses to anyone who asked, meaning it was super cheap to produce, hence the saying: 'Drunk for one penny. Dead drunk for tuppence.'

By 1730, we Brits were all up to our necks in gin, swimming in the midst of the Gin Craze and poor Londoners looking to block out the reality of a miserable, poverty-stricken existence were on average each knocking back about 65 litres a year. The government's attempts to make it harder to sell only resulted in underground brewing of alcohols spiked with poisons to replicate the taste and smell of gin. Londoners were swigging back alcohols laced with turpentine (which smelled similar to juniper), sulphuric acid (to add 'warmth' and 'kick' to replicate the taste of alcohol), caustic potash (to disguise any colourings from the toxins) and a poisonous berry called Coculus indicous, which knocked drinkers into a stupor making them think they were drunk. (Incidentally, it is used as an ointment for scabies as it paralyses the mites, which should give you some indication of why it wasn't an ideal mixer choice.)

By the seventeenth century gin had almost brought London to its knees and was being blamed for misery, rising crime, prostitution, madness, higher death rates and falling birth rates amongst working-class Londoners.

It was also responsible for murder, which is where Judith Defoe comes in. In 1734 Defoe collected her two-year-old child from the workhouse, strangled him, dumped his body in a ditch and sold the clothes he was wearing for 1s and 4d so she could buy herself some gin.

The case, which scandalised London, lead to the origin of the phrase 'Mother's Ruin' and the bad rep as a liquor for drunks that the drink has had ever since.

All terrible stuff, but that was nearly three centuries ago. It really is time to give this liquor a bit of a positive drinking makeover, isn't it?

Although today's gins are not flavoured with turps and acids and poisons, you do still need to have your wits about you to check that you are, in fact, drinking the decent stuff and as healthily as possible. Let's look at what to look for.

Whereas I think there's little point in paying for a massively expensive vodka, as they all taste pretty much the same when served ice cold, with gin it's different. Gins vary in taste and quality massively from brand to brand. Here are some things to look for on the label.

TYPES OF GIN

As a broad guide to choosing a gin that's high in quality and low in sweeteners, look for the words 'London Dry Gin' or 'Plymouth Gin' on the label.

London Dry Gin on a label is not an indicator of where it is made, it means it has been distilled twice during the making. It is 'dry' in that it lacks sugar, making it a better choice for healthier drinking. It mixes well with vermouth so use in Martinis and for a low-sugar gin and tonic.

Plymouth Gin is a clear, slightly fruity, full-bodied gin that is very aromatic. Only one distillery, Plymouth, Coates & Co, has the right to produce Plymouth gin now and because of the strict regulations surrounding this type of liquor, Plymouth gin is always an extremely high quality. Best enjoyed simply poured over ice, with an optional twist of lemon or lime.

Other gins to try, with caution, include:

Old Tom Gin Sweeter than London dry gin, still sold in England and used in some bars. It gives a more rounded taste than London gins, but if a bar has made its own version, check what sugars they've added or you could wake up feeling a bit like the wretched Judith Defoe.

Dutch or Genever or Schiedam Gin This is the Dutch version of gin. It is distilled from malted grain mash similar to whiskey and tends to be lower proof than its English counterparts but it is also more pungent so it is best when paired with strong, sweet flavours that won't be overpowered by its aroma. Its signature cocktail is the 'Sweet City', made with red vermouth and apricot brandy, which frankly sounds very much like a recipe for a hangover.

Sloe Gin Sloe berries, sugar and gin. This should be sipped as a liqueur. Don't go overboard as the sugar will give you a ghastly headache.

TYPES OF BOTANICALS

The flavour of gin is all about the herbs and spices – or botanicals – that are added. By law, gin's main flavour has to come from juniper berries, which smell like a very clean and jolly hamster cage when you smell them in a jar, but which give gin that distinctive pine type hit or 'nip' (a phrase that comes from a shortening of Juniper).

After this there's a myriad of berries, barks, seeds, peels, roots and flowers that can be shoved in to add flavour. Ask the barman what botanicals are used, or check the bottle. There are hundreds of varieties but a glance at the ingredients can give you a clue as to what to expect from your glass: the freshness of orange or lemon peel; the sweetness of honeysuckle; the warm Christmassy spices of cinnamon and cassia bark; floral notes from lavenders or lilacs, the flavours of herbs such as sage or coriander.

It doesn't necessary follow that the more botanicals listed means the better and more expensive the product, but a fine gin will generally contain more than six botanicals. There's one out there, called Monkey 47, that actually contains forty-seven, which is bordering on showing off, but it tastes jolly nice and has a lovely picture of a monkey on the front.

Happily, the best way to decide which gin is right for you is to go to a pub or bar and try a few shots as it's all down to individual tastes and palates.

GIN INSTRUCTORS

As some bars can contain as many as forty different gins, to save you time and save your head, I've enlisted help from a gin instructor to take you through the minefield. Here are some popular brands as recommended by Jake F. Burger, gin historian and gin blender who runs the wonderful Ginstitute museum upstairs at the Portobello Star in London's Portobello Road (portobellostarbar.co.uk).

The following have been stalwarts of the gin world for decades, and understandably so, as they all have impeccable distillation techniques:

> **Plymouth** A unique smooth gin but do watch out for its
> Plymouth Navy strength which comes in at a head-twisting
> 57 per cent ABV. A very fine gin but at that strength it'll knock
> your socks off. Drink it long.

Beefeater Out of all the London-style gins, this is the only globally recognised brand that's still actually made in London. A consistently good-quality gin at 40 per cent ABV.

Portobello Road Gin Jake's own 42 per cent ABV brand developed at his Ginstitute is intended to replicate the original quality gins from yesteryear. Having tried it, I can confirm it is a most agreeable blend of nine botanicals – juniper berries, lemon peel, bitter orange peel, coriander seeds, orris root, angelica root, cassia bark, liquorice and nutmeg. It makes an amazing Martini. (See Jake's recipe on page 120.)

Tanqueray Tanqueray No.10 comes in at a tempestuous 47.3 per cent ABV. Tanqueray's London Dry Gin is an excellent product. Watch the label for ABV though as it changes around the world. The version sold in the UK is 43.1 per cent ABV and is very agreeable. In the US it's a whacking 47.3 per cent ABV and in Canada and Australia 40 per cent ABV.

Other brands to try include:

Citadelle A super-pure distillation system with no sugar added.

Death's Door Gin Nicer than it sounds with its mix of coriander and fennel.

Finsbury London Gin Developed in the eighteenth-century. But its Export Strength is an astonishing 60 per cent ABV so proceed with caution and a pre-booked taxi home.

Hendricks Infused in cucumber and rose petals. (See notes on garnishes on page 108)

Old Raj 55% A saffron-infused gin that is highly rated by barmen and scores brilliantly in professional tasting contests. As the name suggests, this Scottish gin is a startling 55 per cent ABV though.

Sacred Gin Another fine London dry gin whose makers, rather marvellously, have created a gin-flavouring kit to go with it to enable you to create your very own signature gin.

Sipsmith Established in 2009 by Sam Galsworthy and master distiller Jared Brown, this is also an exceptional London dry gin distilled using English barley spirit with a selection of ten botanicals including Macedonian juniper, Bulgarian coriander and Seville orange peel. The result is a particularly dry gin with spicy juniper and a hint of lemon tart emerging.

Right, let's start on the basics. How about a nice gin and tonic?

HOW TO MIX A POSITIVE-DRINKING GIN AND TONIC

Pick your gin according to the rules and tastes, as listed above. I'd go for a nice dry premium London gin and one at around 40 per cent ABV so you get the taste without it smacking you round your senses.

FAQ: And I just get the cheapest tonic I can find in the supermarket do I? After all, it's only water, what difference does it make?

Oh, please tell me you are joking. My tonics masterclass was on page 23. Buy a cheap sugar-laden brand and you'll suffer. Plus why go to all that trouble buying a premium brand to pour in a cheap mix that is going to take up two-thirds of your glass? A good tonic is worth the investment to keep the pristine balance of your drink. Fentimans and Fever-Tree tonics are stocked in most stores and offer very good low-calorie versions. The beauty of these brands, and especially the Waitrose own-brand offering, is that they also all retain their sparkle ensuring a lively happy mix down to the last sip.

FAQ: Alright, so I've got my G&T. So I suppose I just pop in a slice of lime and some ice and I'm done?

Time for a master class on garnishes. Don't just stick a slice of lime in there. The garnish can make all the difference to the final taste of your gin, and needn't add to calories.

As a guide, I'd look at which botanicals are used to flavour the gin and then experiment with trying a new garnish to complement these flavours. For example, if gins are citrusy, then lemon and lime works well or try a slice of blood orange for a change. If it contains warming peppery or spicy flavourings like cinnamon try a twist of grapefruit. The Portobello Road gin, for example, goes wonderfully with a slice of pink grapefruit, which seems to give its spicy cassia bark flavour an extra kick.

If the gin is chiefly of floral botanicals, like camomile or honeysuckle, try strawberries. Try fresh mint leaves with dry London gins.

Hendricks is flavoured with cucumber, so add a slice of cucumber instead of lime. If you are feeling romantic and decadent you can even add frozen rose petals (see recipe page 111).

A slice of fennel or pear does wonders to bring out the flavours in Death's Door gin. If you're drinking pink gins – recipe below – try a sprig of lavender. A couple of dashes of orange bitters mix beautifully with a Plymouth gin; try adding them to Martinis (positive recipe on page 117) to give an extra kick.

There's no hard and fast rule. Just make sure the gin is high quality, not too high an ABV and that the tonic is as healthy as you can find. That will guarantee the least effect on your head in the morning. After that, it's about discovering what tastes you like.

For splendid results, please follow my advice on ice (page 10) and use only clean, clear ice. For extra staying power, use crushed ice to serve gins that are over 40 per cent ABV so that the ice quickly dissolves, bringing down its strength.

'I used to jog but the ice cubes kept falling out of my glass.'
David Lee Roth

So, let's do a few positive gin cocktail makeovers, shall we?

POSITIVE PINK GIN & TONIC
35ml London dry gin
Waitrose sugar-free tonic water
A few drops of Angostura bitters
Sprig of lavender or a handful of frozen raspberries
Ice

Pour the bitters over the ice, add your gin, and top up with the tonic
water. Stir with the lavender sprig or drop in the raspberries and serve.

TANQUERAY

5 slices English cucumber
1 unpeeled lime, cut in eighths (bitter white centre pith removed)
Handful of fresh herbs – I love a mixture of basil, lemon thyme,
tarragon, lavender, mint, and a touch of rosemary
50ml Tanqueray London dry gin
Waitrose sugar-free tonic water
Pinch salt
Twist freshly cracked pepper

In a jug, combine cucumbers, lime and herbs; muddle until juicy and
aromatic. Add the Tanqueray London dry gin, stir, fill with ice, top with
tonic, and stir again. Pour into a 16-ounce pint glass rimmed with the
salt and pepper. Garnish with cucumber slices and fresh herbs.

SUMMER GIN AND TONIC

35ml gin
Four drops of grapefruit bitters
Waitrose sugar-free tonic water

Pour ice into a long glass, dash the bitters over the glass,
pour in the gin and top up with tonic water.

ROSE GIN AND TONIC

I pint filtered water

Handful washed and torn rose petals

50ml Hendricks gin

Cucumber

Waitrose sugar-free tonic water

Pour the filtered water into an ice-cube tray, scatter in the washed rose petals and leave to freeze overnight. Then top a glass with the rose cubes and make a gin and tonic with Hendricks, garnished with cucumber slices. Hendricks is flavoured with cucumber and rose petals so the additions enhance its flavourings – and look jolly pretty if there's someone you're trying to impress.

LOW-SUGAR GIMLET MARTINI

Juice of one freshly squeezed lime

Dash organic agave syrup

50ml Plymouth gin

Lime wedges

Splash chilled water

Fill a tall mixing glass with ice, pour in the fresh lime and gin, add a splash of chilled water, stir and strain into a Martini glass. Add the lime wedges to decorate. Recipes often call for lime cordial to be used instead of fresh limes and organic agave syrup, but check the sugar content of the mixer before using to avoid taking on hidden calories. Many brands are a lurid green from food colourings and contain mountains of sweeteners.

The term 'limeys' to describe Brits comes from the sailors' habit of drinking lime-based drinks to up their vitamin C intake and ward off scurvy. However, due to the manufacturing process, the vitamin C content of lime cordials can actually be tiny. Much better to use fresh limes, which are now available all year round with a dash of organic agave syrup to add a healthy natural low-GI sweetener.

LOW-SUGAR BEEFEATER FLORIDA 75

(adapted from the official recipe on the Beefeater gin website, www.ginandtales.com)

40ml Beefeater 24 gin
20ml freshly squeezed pink grapefruit juice
10ml organic agave syrup
Brut or Ultra Brut Champagne
Grapefruit peel

Shake the gin, grapefuit juice and agave together over ice, strain into a champagne flute, top up with dry champagne and garnish with a grapefuit twist.

LOW-SUGAR CITRUS CRUSH

*(adapted from the official recipe on the
Beefeater gin website, www.ginandtales.com)*

50ml Beefeater gin
20ml freshly squeezed lemon juice
Dash of organic agave syrup
Ice

Pour all the ingredients into a blender with ice and whizz up to create a smoothie. This will bring the alcohol content of the double shot of gin down and create a longer drink. To make an even longer drink, do not blend, but pour into a long glass and top with two shots of low-sugar tonic water.

You can also try throwing more fruit into the blender mix to create fruit-based smoothies. But always keep the base of two shots of gin, lemon juice and organic agave syrup to create a refreshing kick. Try throwing in a few slices of watermelon or a few strawberries. Adding fruit is much healthier than adding fruit liquours.

You can also substitute gin for tequila in my original positive Margarita recipe:

50ml London gin
Juice of two fresh limes
Dash of organic agave syrup

Shake the ingredients over ice and garnish with mint. But do watch the alcohol content of the gin. I certainly don't guarantee hangover-free drinking if you start knocking back the 57 per cent ABV stuff as part of this cocktail.

LEMON ICED TEA

50ml London gin
75ml of English breakfast tea, chilled – and I presume you'll figure out that you don't add milk or sugar
15ml of organic agave syrup
Juice of half a fresh lemon

Fill a tall glass with ice and pour in the tea, agave syrup and gin, stir, add a squeeze of fresh lemon and sip.

These next three recipes work beautifully with a Scottish gin called Caorunn (www.caorunningin.com), which, as well as Heather, bog myrtle and dandelion botanicals, contains celtic apple.

CAORUNN APPLE TWIST

50ml Caorunn gin
100ml pressed apple juice
200ml Fentimans tonic water

Add cubed ice to glass, add gin, apple juice and then tonic. Stir after adding thinly sliced apple and lemon.

CAORUNN APPLE SMASH

50ml Caorunn gin

200ml Fentimans tonic water

¼ red apple

¼ green apple

2 cloves

Muddle the quartered apples into the Caorunn Gin in a cocktail shaker. Add the cloves and shake all together. Strain over cubed ice and top up a long glass with the tonic water.

CAORUNN BLUSH

50ml Caorunn gin

200ml Fentimans tonic water

2 dashes Angostura bitters

Add cubed ice to glass, add gin, tonic and bitters. Stir thinly sliced apple and lemon into the glass.

STORING YOUR GIN

As with vodka, you can shove your bottles in the freezer to stay cold. It will not freeze. Again, keep the top of the bottle on to avoid evaporation.

FAQ: What if I get a bottle of gin that's a bit rough? Should I just throw it away?

If you've been gifted a bottle of gin that tastes a little rough, trying filtering it through a Britta water filter. This will result in a smoother-tasting spirit. This also helps if people present you with their rough homemade sloe gin and then insist on staying to watch you drink it.

SERVING YOUR GIN

Although a tall glass is traditional, consider serving a gin and tonic in a large balloon glass. It can help the tonic keep its sparkle, and helps the garnish infuse with the drink.

MAKING A GIN MARTINI

'A perfect Martini should be made by filling a glass with gin then waving it in the general direction of Italy.'
Noel Coward

There are those who say Martinis should only ever be made with gin and that vodka Martinis are an evil imposter. Personally, I rather enjoy both. But a gin Martini was the original, so let's look at how to serve that.

The first thing to bear in mind about a gin Martini, is the strength of the gin. So if you're making the following with anything that's over 40 per cent ABV then only do it if you're not out in public, or don't have to say anything important to anyone for the rest of the day. It is also an excellent drink when you've just had a row with someone and wish to pour them something quickly to shut them up and calm them down. Or if someone you don't like much is visiting and you want them to go to bed early.

EMERGENCY GIN MARTINI
50ml gin (straight from the freezer)
The merest drop of dry vermouth
Lemon rind

Simply pour the vermouth into the gin, stir and serve. This drink is best enjoyed ice cold and will stay ice cold for about four minutes so try to drink it in this timescale. Two of them should be enough to send even the most unwelcome guest into an agreeable slumber.

As with vodka Martinis this mix is absolute rocket fuel.

I'd say no more than two in one evening because as Dorothy Parker famously declared: I like to have a Martini, two at the very most. After three I'm under the table, after four I'm under my host.

There is a way of drinking it that won't lead to you being flat out on the shag pile. Let's look at making it a little less potent.

POSITIVE GIN MARTINI
50ml London Dry Gin at no more than 40 per cent ABV
e.g. Beefeater
30ml vermouth
Lemon or olive to garnish

This mix brings the ABV of the Martini down by choosing a weaker gin and makes a 'wetter' Martini – i.e. decrease the gin and increase the vermouth. Vermouth is only 15 per cent ABV so increasing the amount will knock the ABV down. I know that with vodka Martinis I advocated the merest whisper of vermouth, but as gin has much more flavour I think you can get away with a little more vermouth, and a little less gin in the mixture, in order to improve your staying power.

Using an ice shaker will help things even more. Shake the mix in a cocktail shaker filled with ice and the ice will dilute it further, bringing you down another percentage or two. If serving at home at a dinner party, then mix up a batch that covers a cocktail each, pour everyone a half measure in their glass for them to sip, then after a few minutes top up from the shaker as the ice has started to melt inside.

Prepared this way, then, over an evening you can sip three Martinis for the same alcohol content as the two rocket-fuelled Martinis straight from the freezer. To add an extra kick to the weakened gin mix, try adding a couple of splashes of flavoured bitters.

FAQ: As I only use a drop of vermouth at a time I have a bottle in the cupboard which I've had for years. Will this do?

No.

Vermouth is a wine. So it is important to remember that it goes off just like wine. So invest in a vacuum pump for it. Or throw it away after a month, three months at the most if you keep it in the fridge.

If a bar boasts of having had the same vermouth bottle for decades because it serves its drinks so dry, then for goodness' sake don't touch it. It went off years ago.

COCKTAILS OF THE NINETEENTH CENTURY

The 'wetter' style of Martini is how the drink was originally served and old-style recipes show drinks were originally mixed as half and half of the weaker vermouths to liquor.

Here's a recipe for the original gin Martini taken from the *Jerry Thomas' Bartenders Guide*, which was a Mrs Beeton for bartenders brought out in the nineteenth century. You can read it all online free at www.artofdrink.com/jerry-thomas/ or ask Jake nicely at the Ginstitute and he'll show you his copy.

ORIGINAL GIN MARTINI
2 or 3 dashes of gum syrup
2 or 3 dashes of bitters
1 dash of curacao or absinthe
Half wine glass of Old Tom gin
Half wine glass of vermouth

Stir up well with a spoon, strain into a chilled cocktail glass,
put in a cherry or medium-sized olive and squeeze a
slice of lemon peel on top and serve.

Absinthe and gin? This is one chap who didn't mess around when it came to drinks. Here's a Modern-Day Positive makeover of his drink.

A POSITIVE NINETEENTH-CENTURY MARTINI

(With thanks to Jake Burger)
2 or 3 dashes organic agave syrup
2 or 3 dashes of Bob's (Abbott's) Bitters
one shot of London dry gin
one shot vermouth

Stir up well with a spoon, strain into a chilled fancy cocktail glass,
serve with orange peel

Bob's Bitters, by the way, are available at www.thewhiskyexchange.com and are a modern-day recreation of the bartender's ingredient Abbott's Bitters, which was sold in the nineteenth century. It was developed by the pastry chef at the the Dorchester Hotel in London, Robert Petrie, and Jake at the Ginstitute who bought an unopened bottle of the Bitters dating back to 1920 and managed to analyse its contents using gas chromatography techniques. All very complicated, the good news for us is that all we have to do is shake a couple of drops into cocktails to recreate old-fashioned tastes.

The Whiskey Exchange, which ships around the world, sells a series of flavoured bitters such as grapefruit or orange, which can be used to replace citrus-flavoured liqueurs in drinks to cut down on sugars. They all cost less than £20 a bottle and last for years.

'Martini. Shaken, not stirred.'
James Bond

'James Bond may be many things, but a positive drinker he is not. When you look at how he has his Martinis it's no wonder he spends half of every movie flat on his back.'
Cleo Rocos

THE JAMES BOND VESPER MARTINI
50ml London Gin
15ml vodka
5ml Lillet Blanc French vermouth (made with white wines
and fruit brandy)
lemon peel garnish

And probably an aspirin or two in the morning. Still, at least our hero did make one concession to positivity. By shaking it, he will have brought down the ABV a percentage point or two, which enabled him to keep hold of that license to kill.

FAQ: What do I do with really bad gin that doesn't even improve with filtering?

Do not throw it away. Gin, even the really rough stuff, is an excellent cleaner for diamonds. A fact noted by Her Majesty's favourite jewellers, Garrard of Bond St, London. Though one does wonder how the gin and jewellery came to meet in the first place in the royal household.

'The only time I ever enjoyed ironing was the day
I accidentally got gin in the steam iron.'
Phyllis Diller

'Of all the gin joints in all the towns in all the world,
she walks into mine.'
Humphrey Bogart

'Ah, but it's being able to walk out again with grace
that's the key, Mr B.'
Cleo Rocos

HERE'S LOOKING AT YOU, KID. WELL, THAT'S GIN
COVERED. ANYONE FANCY A WHISKY CHASER?

LESSON EIGHT

HOW TO AVOID RISKY WHISKY

(AND SURVIVE UNSCATHED FROM THE VILLAGE OF THE DRAMMED)

'I've had eighteen straight whiskies, I think that's a record!'
Dylan Thomas' last words

*'Well, in the afterlife maybe give it a go the way
I'm about to describe.'*
Cleo Rocos

've had some wonderous times on whisky. The divine Kenny
Everett used to greatly enjoy a straight shot of Cragganmore as
we laughed our way through filming sketches. And I once had a
magical evening doing high kicks to Ethel Merman show tunes with
Gore Vidal as we roared through his whisky collection in Ravello. But
more of that later.

First the bad news. Whisky is at least 40 per cent ABV and contains
more hangover-inducing congener chemicals than clear liquors like
vodka or gin. So by drinking it, you could well end up in a vortex of
horror.

A bad whisky hangover is truly an act of evil upon your body.
It is dreadful. I've been lucky enough to escape fairly unscathed after sipping some of the world's finest whiskies, but generally, if you're doing a night on it, you'll wake feeling like you've left your brains on the pillow and with a dead donkey rotting in your throat. It's like going a few rounds with Muhammed Ali, except that whilst it stings like a bee on your taste buds, it will also float like a rhino on your forehead the next morning.

Unless you limit yourself to a glass or two there's no way you can emerge unscathed the next day. And frankly, what's the fun in that?

The main problem with the stuff is the way whisky purists insist you drink it.

Neat

And that's about it.

Purists say you should pour a dram of whisky into a glass, swirl it around vigorously then chuck the whole lot out onto the carpet to 'cleanse' the glass of impurities, before pouring another dram into the glass.

You should then stick your nose in the glass and inhale deeply at least three times before taking a sip and hold it on the tongue for one second for every year of its age.

Then, and only then are you allowed to swallow.

I find whisky purists get very upset if you deviate from this. They start tutting if you add ice and go apoplectic at the thought of soda water or mixers. At the very, very most, they'll allow you the tiniest drop of filtered water.

Ignore them

Drink it however you wish. It's your whisky, and it's your head the next day. Besides, if you're going to have a hangover you may as well enjoy acquiring it.

You don't allow someone to turn up at your breakfast table and tell you how to toast your toast, do you? You have your tea how you like your tea. Would you really listen to someone who turned up and dictated which precise vegetables should be consumed with your Sunday roast to derive maximum pleasure? No. So why meekly obey the rules when it comes to whisky?

Drink is about enjoying yourself, relaxing and having fun. Not being preached to. Besides, whisky experts can't even agree on how it should be spelled, never mind consumed. Half of them argue it's spelled 'whiskey', the other half 'whisky'. For the record, as a general rule it's whisky for those brands distilled in Scotland, Wales, Canada and Japan, and 'whiskey' elsewhere. Or at least it was at the time of writing. Somebody has probably argued something different by now. Just in case the spelling offends you here are a few spare e's you can cut out and paste into the copy: Eeeeeeeeeeeeeeeeeeeeeeeeeeeeeeeeee eeeeeeeeeeeeeeeeeeeeeeeeeeeeeeeee

Whilst you get on with that I'm going to pour a drink.

First up, the idea of throwing whisky on your carpet is silly. Just give the glass you're drinking from a really good rinse in water and a polish and the whisky will taste just fine.

If someone is rude enough to start hurling whisky all over your carpets then you really don't have to listen to them. Whisky costs money, as does dry cleaning the carpet afterwards. And, frankly, it's rude to offer soft furnishings the same libation as your guests. Secondly, should you ever get into an argument with a whisky purist don't worry too much because it won't last long. Pretty soon they'll be in no fit state to argue with you because they're hurtling head first to Hangover Hell.

Just get on and enjoy it. You don't need to sit there dipping your nose in. Drink it. See if you like it. Pretty straightforward, really.

Now let's really annoy the purists. Let's tamper with it and give it a 'Positive Makeover'.

When it comes to whisky, do as the Japanese do.

The Japanese love whisky. They drink it as an aperitif, with their meal, and after their meal as a digestif and yet remain svelte and gracious and still able to shuffle home in their kimonos. Although some of those geisha girls do look like they've applied their make-up after a few drams.

Their tradition is not to drink it straight, but to drink it as a *Mizuwari*.

A Mizuwari translates as 'mixed with water' and typically involves two parts of cold water to one part spirits, plus ice. Everything the whisky purists howl about basically. But it's delicious.

It also has the advantage of working rather brilliantly with the younger, less expensive whiskies so it's less impact on your wallet as well as your head.

Give this recipe for a whisky *Mizuwari* a try. I've mixed it with a beautiful Japanese whisky called Hibiki 17 Year Old, which costs around £69 a bottle and is 43 per cent ABV.

POSITIVE WHISKY *MIZUWARI*

25ml Hibiki 17 Year Old whisky
50–75ml chilled mineral water
Two large ice cubes made of frozen mineral water or an ice ball*
(* For guidance on the best ice to use see page 10)

According to traditional Japanese Mizuwari-making rituals, you should add the whisky to the ice, stir thirteen and a half times clockwise, then add the water and stir a further three and a half times to blend.

The stirring bit is up to you but do make sure you give it all a quick muddle around and the result is a beautiful chilled drink that retains the flavours of the original whisky blend, but is younger, fresher, easier on the head and much, much nicer to have as a drink alongside food. It goes wonderfully well with fish, meats and lamb. Purists may hate it being watered down, but served this way you remove the tongue-burning effect of the original, and taste the lighter notes of cherries and butterscotch in the whisky.

Plus the resulting drink can last for a good hour, sipped as a long, chilled cordial, and a night out drinking whisky in this way will have far less effect on the head. I've spoken to bartenders who cheerfully admit to having gone into double figures on these on a night out and made it through intact.

Other Japanese whiskies to look for which taste superb consumed this way are **Yamazaki 12 Year Old** and **Hakushu 12 Year Old**.

Both come in under the £50 mark and you get twenty-eight shots and therefore twenty-eight long drinks out of the bottle if you prepare it this way, so it doesn't prove too damaging on the wallet.

Ginger Ale can be used instead of water in the same proportions, with a wedge of orange added as a twist. However, check the label as some ginger ale brands can be laden with sugar, which means a greater hangover and a more fattening drink. I'd recommend Naturally Light Ginger Ale, which has just been launched in the Fever-Tree mixers range and can be bought in good supermarkets.

FAQ: What about whisky and cola? That's a good mixer, isn't it? Makes me look tough too.

Oh dear no. Absolutely not. Always say no to cola. All brands. Diet or otherwise.

Not only are you totally masking the taste of the whisky but the sugar and chemicals that go into a cola mean you're definitely drinking a hangover in a glass. It's your choice, obviously, but bartenders wince on your behalf when they serve you this muck because they know what your morning will be like.

The only acceptable time to mix a whisky with cola is if you're making it for someone you really don't like.

FAQ: How do I store my whisky?

Again, purists will probably kill me here for even suggesting this, but apart from storing it in your drinks cabinet, some maverick and avant-garde mixologists suggest that you might try storing it in your freezer.

This enables you to try an ice-cold sip to acquaint yourself with the tastes, which will develop and open up as the drink warms up. A cold whisky will reveal different flavours to a room-temperature whisky. The beauty of drinking it this way is that if you have teenage kids or freeloading guests around they are less likely to find the bottles and drink it.

The following positive cocktail was created for this book by leading mixologist Zoran Peric who was kind enough to introduce me to the rules and rituals of *Mizuwari*. Again, save your wallet as this tastes just as nice with the cheaper whiskies. He recommends the Hakushu 12 Year Old.

ELDERFLOWER WHISKY
Chilled tumbler glass
Two large pieces of ice
35ml Belvoir elderflower cordial
50ml Hakushu 12 Year Old whisky
Soda water
Lemon zest
Sprig of elderflower blossom

Throw the cracked ice in the tumbler, coat it with a shot of Belvoir elderflower cordial and a large measure of Hakushu 12 Year Old whisky. Top the glass with soda water, and garnish with lemon zest and elderflower blossom. The result is summertime in a glass and minimal heat in your head the next morning.

'Love makes the world go round? Not at all.
Whisky makes it go round twice as fast.'
Compton Mackenzie

'Not necessarily, noodle, just keep the water flowing too.'
Cleo Rocos

Oh, and as described on page 83, to maximise your chances of surviving unscathed, never, ever drink whisky with bores.

As a perfect example of a night out on whisky, let me tell you about a delightful cocktail hour with Gore Vidal.

GORE VIDAL
Adventures in Whisky

One of my most favourite and indeed most divinely memorable experiences involving whisky took place in the magical town of Ravello, Italy. I was filming my fantastic travel/interview TV series and was there with the lovely Denise van Outen, who was my guest for that particular episode.

I had been introduced to the beyond-enigmatic and giant of a man Gore Vidal by my great and dear friend Nicky Haslam. Gore lived in Ravello and invited Denise and me to his glorious house for cocktails. As the sun hit the horizon, we wrapped the filming for the day and off Denise and I went to Gore's house. A long pathway with a series of gates eventually led us to his magnificent home, which was in possession of the most heavenly and incredible views. It was crammed to the brim with objects of beauty and amazing priceless works of art.

He was truly fabulous and greeted us with great warmth and enthusiasm. Gore was a wonderful host and was extremely generous with what seemed to be a most rare vintage bottle of whisky. He poured us each a whisky and soda and we sat chatting animatedly about all sorts of scandalous goings-on, past and present. From Princess Diana's demise to the Kennedys', Rock Hudson, Elizabeth Taylor and James Dean. I was intrigued to learn that Gore Vidal was related to Al Gore. It seems that they were distant cousins.

Gore opened a drawer in his large desk and produced the most beautiful photos of himself and all the fashionable movie stars, handsome young writers and politicians of the day. Photos of them all on a holidays together having a wonderful time in the fifties and sixties. Every random shot of them on the beach and having fun was exquisite. They looked so stylish and as though they had fallen off a *Vogue* cover together and were caught in a moment of sheer perfection.

As Gore and I enjoyed his fine bottle of whisky we became more and more excited in conversation, and I could see that Denise was possibly a little distracted. Gore and I were like old chums. I had commented that his enormous fireplace resembled a small theatre stage. He agreed and as Ethel Merman belted out show tunes in the background I felt compelled to jump up and do high kicks in his fireplace. He delighted in this and we shrieked with laughter. We spent hours besotted and illegally happy in outrageous conversation. Then suddenly, as he put his glass to his lips, it was empty and so was the bottle . . . 'You bitch,' he cried. 'You've drunk all the whisky.' Then he roared with laughter. 'Cleo, you didn't see that coming,' he bellowed mischievously.

I can assure you that we drank the bottle between us and he did put a little more of a dent into it than I did. I absolutely loved him. I hoped that Denise had enjoyed meeting him as much as I had.

A few weeks later I received a phone call from Nicky. He was beside himself with laughter and reeling in delight as he relayed the story of how Denise had been recounting her time in Ravello and had declared how much she had enjoyed meeting Vidal Sassoon . . . I roared with laughter. Well, Gore, you didn't see that coming!

POSITIVE CLUB WHISKY

50ml bourbon whisky

Half-slice fresh orange

1 tsp organic agave syrup

2 dashes Angostura aromatic bitters

Lemon twist

Splash water

Add ice to the first five ingredients and stir well.
Top with a splash of water.

FAQ: Is there any way I can turn cheap whisky into something drinkable?

Even some of the cheapest whiskies can be transformed by adding one shot of sweet vermouth to two shots of whisky. Add a dash of Angostura bitters and shake over ice and it will result in a passable Manhattan. Serve it to the person who gave it to you in the first place, though, and let them have the hangover.

FAQ: So, what whisky should I buy?

As a general rule, respect your elders: age is good.

'I like my whisky old and my women young.'
Errol Flynn

Look for a number on the bottle, which indicates how long the whisky has been aged for before bottling. Generally speaking, the higher the number, the more expensive, and better, it is.

Legally a Scotch or Irish whisky, for example, need only be aged for three years, but once it is aged for ten, twelve or eighteen years it means the maker has done more work to add character and flavour. The older the drink the smoother it tends to be too, although unfortunately it will also be more expensive. Think of the cheap whisky as a groupie and the expensive as a Sophia Loren. The first may not cost so much to win their affections, but has a bad aftertaste and you'll be full of regrets in the morning. With Sophia, she may be far less affordable but you're in for an exquisite, elegant and most memorable evening that you'll savour and want to relive.

Where the whisky is a blend of whiskies and an age is specified it means the spirits that have been blended are at least that old.

With whisky, as with gin, it's a case of finding something to suit your palate and a way to drink it that appeals. Here is a rough guide to some of the things out there to help you work through all the labels.

Malt whisky Generally speaking, this has a more robust flavour.

Grain whisky A lighter, smoother style of whisky.

Blended whisky A mix of the two. The maker does not have to reveal what proportions of whiskies are used, but if an age is displayed it means that is the youngest whisky contained in the product so it will give you an idea of quality.

Cask Strength whisky (or barrel proof). A mark of quality as it is bottled from the cask undiluted. Only the best are produced this way.

'No married man is genuinely happy if he has to drink worse whisky than he used to drink when he was single.'
H. L. Mencken

A QUICK GUIDE TO BRANDS

When buying Scotch or Irish whisky as a general guide look for anything aged over ten years, which will have taken on more of the characteristics of the individual brand.

A broad guide to **Scotch** flavours:

Highlands: spicy, smoky, and sherry-like. E.g., Glenmorangie.

Lowlands: dry, light, non smoky. Good for aperitifs or those not used to whisky. E.g., Glenkinchie.

Speyside: complex and sweet. E.g., Glenfarclas 15 Year Old.

Islay: smokey and intense with a peat kick that will whack you around the chin. E.g., Ardbeg and Caol Ila.

For Irish try the Kilbeggan blend, which comes in around the £20 mark and is made by the only Irish-owned independent distillery, Cooley.

Bourbon American Whiskey. There is no minimum specification for ageing, but a bourbon that has been aged for a minimum of two years, and does not have added colouring, flavouring or other spirits, can be labelled as straight bourbon. A Tennessee-style whisky is straight bourbon whisky produced in Tennessee, such as Jack Daniel's. Do not mix it with cola because otherwise you'll be on your way to a sugar and chemical hell of a hangover. Try instead one shot of bourbon to three shots of low-sugar ginger ale.

We'd be here for ever trying to go through all the brands, so here, instead, is a quick guide to buying whisky, depending on the amount of trouble you're in, or how much you wish to attempt to charm the recipient.

I'm in minor trouble with my boss/I need to thank a neighbour for looking after my pet/I have been invited to meet the parents of my date and will go to be polite, but I'm not sure she's a keeper.

A very polite, yet reasonably priced thank-you is a Johnnie Walker Black Label 12 Year Old for around £25. Or a Black Bushmills Irish Whiskey will come in at under £25 and will be gratefully received without breaking the bank.

I'm in medium-level trouble with the boss/I'm really sorry about what my pet did to the person's sofa who was looking after it/I am somewhat keen to seduce my new date and she has invited me to supper with her parents so I need to impress.

Hmmm, you want something of quality for just under £50. Try an older reliable blended whisky, such as a Balvenie Single Barrel 15 Year Old. A Clynelish 14 Year Old, an Oban 14

Year Old, a Caol Ila 12 Year Old, a Glenfarclas 15 Year Old or a Talisker 10 Year Old are also choices which scream effort. Hopefully they'll share a glass with you.

I have done major damage to my boss's car/ I've done something in front of the boss at his dinner party that will involve a dry-cleaning bill/I've lost or killed my neighbour's pet/my date's parents hate me but I'm still intending to propose to her.

You had better start looking at the bottles labelled 'rarest vintage reserve'. Pick a dram to match the crime. The most expensive whisky ever sold was a sixty-four-year-old Macallan single malt, which went for £288,000 at Sotheby's in 2010. Now that really was a good apology. In emergencies it may be cheaper simply to move house.

'Friendship is like whisky: the older, the better.'
Anon

'Whisky, like a beautiful woman, demands appreciation. You gaze first, then it's time to drink.'
Haruki Murakami

'And like most women, we also appreciate a little staying power. So let's splash in a little mixer so we can all last a little longer.'
Cleo Rocos

RIGHT. RUM?

LESSON NINE

WHAT THEY KEEP SCHTUM ABOUT RUM

'I prefer rum . . . rum's good.'
Captain Jack Sparrow

'Yes, my little Jolly Roger, rum is good . . . for giving you a throbbing hangover. Let's see what I can do.'
Cleo Rocos

So rum's your poison – and poison can be the operative word, given rum is usually created from industrial waste. But, hey, if a Daquiri is exactly what you feel like, then it's your choice. Let's look and see if there's any way of making things a little easier on the skull and bones the next day.

> **FAQ: So what's this about industrial waste? What is rum actually made of?**

There are two sorts of rum: Rhum Agricole or Rhum Industriel/Traditionnel (Agricultural rum and Traditional Industrial rum).

RUM INDUSTRIEL

Industrial rum represents about 90 per cent of the world production of rum and is made from a waste product – molasses. Molasses is the brown stuff left behind by sugar plantations after they've boiled down their sugar cane and produced sugar crystals. This is then fermented and becomes rum. Examples include:

Mount Gay
Mahiki
Havana Club
Diplomatico
El Dorado

RUM AGRICOLE

This method of production is more rare but common in the French West Indies, particularly Martinique. It is rum made from fresh pressed sugar cane juice. Although this method won't make a session on the rum any easier on your head the next day, it has the slight advantage for novice rum buyers in that it is subject to the French Appellation d'Origine Contrôlée or AOC mark, so at least you know if you see that on a bottle then it's a mark that its production methods have been regulated by the French government. A few examples include:

Clément
J.Bally
Rhum J.M.
La Favorite Blanc
Neisson
Flor de Caña Extra Dry White
Saint-James

The problem with rum is that you've got sugar from the start. It's a sweet drink, so you're inevitably hurtling full speed towards a hangover from the first sip. Add to that a myriad different rum makers out there, all in different countries with different rules of production, and you can end up swimming through a sea of confusion.

But there is one positive rule that I can give you: **To drink a rum which will have the least possible effect on you the next day you're looking for something white and old**.

Think a sort of Hugh Heffner of the rum world.

Let me explain. A young rum will be clear. If the maker then goes to the cost and trouble of ageing it to improve the flavour, then it will take on colouring from the barrel. But this ageing process can add impurities called congeners, which are chemicals that occur during fermentation. These can make your hangover much worse the next day. In addition, some unscrupulous producers pump in a load of caramel flavouring to give it colour and the impression that it's older than it is – a sort of fake tan for rum if you will.

The best makers of aged white rum will then pass the aged alcohol through a charcoal filtration process. But as the impurities will be removed, so is the colour. Remember: if the bottle is marked as aged X years or *anejo* or aged, but the liquid inside is clear, then it's a rum that has all of the benefits of being aged, but a lot of the bad stuff has been removed.

Do be careful on age, though. The bottle must be marked 'Aged X Years', as some makers merely stick a number into the brand name to make it look as if they've aged it for that amount of time when they haven't.

Some lovely and trusted examples to look for:

El Dorado 3 Year Old
Toz White Gold (aged 7 years)
Flor de Caña 4 Year Extra Dry
Havana Club Anejo Blanco Rum

Incidentally, if you have a darkly coloured rum at home that you love the taste of it but it gives you a raging hangover, try running a measure through your Britta water filter. It can work wonders. Rum purists may howl that you're removing some of the taste, but if it lets you function the next day, I say go for it.

Let's see what else is out there:

GOLD RUM OR DARK RUMS

These are a bit like Russian roulette unless you stick to the best brands. Technically, the darker the colour, the older the rum should be. But as I've mentioned, so many just cheat and throw caramel or colourings in there, it's hard to tell which have been lovingly tended for years and which are a wolf in sheep's clothing. The only way to tell is to check the bottle for the rum's age.

Gold rums can be used in cocktails and some of my recommended brands include:

El Dorado 12 Year Old
Appleton VX or Reserve
Smith & Cross
Mount Gay Eclipse

The darker the rum, the sweeter it is going to be, so although gold- or amber-coloured rums will work in cocktails, I'd avoid using the really dark ones. Serve them up straight or over ice (if you're sunning your particles on the deck of a luxury yacht), and just sip as you would a brandy or a whisky.

Be it white or dark if it is truly a quality, well-aged rum, then it will be fine to sip and to serve in long or short drinks.

The average house pour rum is what you really want to be very wary of. A consistently good basic rum is Mount Gay. Other brands may be more familiar to you and much more heavily advertised but I have spent a lot of time in the Caribbean and as a house pour, most bartenders who know their rums tend to agree with me on this.

Recommended dark brands include:

Zaya 12 Year
Zacapa 15 or 23 Year
Mount Gay Extra Old
Pampero Aniversario

Even darker and heavier still are **blackstrap** rums made from dark, thick molasses. Good luck in trying to drink these without your head feeling as though it is lodged in the buttocks of all your worst nightmares the next day. Some more favourable brands are:

Cruzan Black Strap
Captain Morgan Black Spiced Rum

On the subject of **spiced rums**, be very careful about what you're buying. These can be laced with artificial flavours, which will really make you feel vile the next day. If you are keen to try these then I suggest trying:

Kraken
Cruzan 9
Sailor Jerry
Doorly's

OVERPROOF RUM

Overproof rums are generally above 120 proof, or 60 per cent ABV and personally I'd avoid them like the plague. I cannot willingly recommend drinking anything over 40 per cent ABV unless you intend to have a limb removed without an anesthetic. When we go out socialising we're not used to being served up anything over 40 per cent ABV, so you can find yourself in all kinds of trouble if you are throwing this strength of shot into a cocktail. This is more for the rum experts and is an acquired taste indeed. There are plenty of fine quality rums out there with a lower ABV. In case you are curious, though, here are some samples of overproof rums:

Goslings 75.5 per cent ABV – Bermuda
Green Island 75.5 per cent ABV – Mauritius
Wray and Nephew 63 per cent ABV – Jamaica

FAQ: So how do I read a rum label?

Strength

As I said before, double check the ABV, a rum is typically 37.5 per cent ABV but do tread carefully as some can soar up to a deliriously and blindingly high 85 per cent ABV. **There's no harm in me saying this again: avoid drinking spirits over 40 per cent ABV.**

Ageing

Check it says 'Aged X Years'. 'Rhum vieux' is good and means it's been aged for at least three years in small barrels in the French islands. 'Anejo', meaning old and 'Gran anejo', meaning even older, again aren't defined by law, but are usually good indications that it's been well looked after. If it's a French Caribbean distiller look for 'vieux', which will mean it's been aged for three years; 'tres vieux', which means even older, and 'hors d'age' means a blend of old rums.

AOC

If it's a Rhum Agricole and marked AOC on the label, this will denote that its production process has been regulated.

Right, let's give a few popular rum-based drinks my positive-drinking makeover, shall we?

Spiced Rum

Throw a few ripe fresh pineapple pieces into the rum bottle (you may need to take a slurp out the top to create room), let it infuse for a few days, then strain into a clean jar and you have a lovely flavoured rum-base for daiquiris.

DAIQUIRI
35ml blanco aged rum
Juice of one fresh squeezed lime
15ml organic agave syrup
Lots of ice

Shake well and pour into a glass, best served on the rocks.

The homemade pineapple spiced rum (above) makes a lovely twist on this.

THE DARK AND STORMY

Usually a killer of a drink because it contains black rum
and sugar syrups. Let's give it a makeover to create less of a storm,
more a pleasurable downpour.

25ml fresh lime juice
25ml Black Seal rum
Fever-Tree low-sugar ginger beer

Add ice to a tall glass, squeeze in lime, fill glass three-quarters full of ginger
beer, then slowly drizzle the rum in over the back of a spoon so it floats on
the top. If you want it sweeter add in a tiny bit of organic agave syrup, but
really, the sweetness of the black rum is usually enough.

TI PUNCH

Ti Punch is a traditional aperitif of the French Antilles. Usually,
bartenders will bring a bottle of punch, a tray of cut limes, and ice and
sugar laid out on a plate, which the drinker then mixes to taste. I've
substituted the usual recipe of 1 ½ teaspoons of brown sugar for organic
agave syrup, but the concept remains the same.

POSITIVE TI PUNCH
ice cubes
35ml aged white rum
10ml fresh lime juice
5ml organic agave syrup

Place ice cubes in glass. Add the rum and lime juice.
Add the agave syrup to taste. Stir.

FAQ: Should I mix rum with cola?

Oh, please don't. You're just adding huge amounts of sugar and chemicals to sweetness and you'll be putting on weight in a showbiz minute, spreading and bursting all over the place. To be avoided!

FAQ: Should I drink rum punch at parties?

Not unless you enjoy waking up in a skip. However, I am indebted to Jules Gauldoni, former mixologist at the Mahiki nightclub in Mayfair, London, the developer of Mahiki Rum and current bar manager at the Cliff Restaurant in Barbados, for this Positive Rum Punch.

He is currently serving it to chic and stylish holidaymakers to sip before dinner as they watch the Carribean waves wash in at St James – nice work if you can get it. It's a replica of Pimm's with lemonade, so much easier on the head than a standard punch, and it's rather gorgeous:

POSITIVE BAJAN GARDEN PUNCH

Stainless-steel jug

3 slices of cucumber

2 slices of lemon

2 slices of orange

2 slices of apple

50ml Mount Gay Eclipse

75ml apple juice

15ml elderflower liquor (St Germain)

Put the cucumber and fruit in the jug with one mint sprig and one sprig of fresh marjoram, muddle gently. Add the rum, apple juice and elderflower liquor. Stir gently and pour into a wine glass over ice

Top up with low-sugar ginger ale and garnish with summer fruits.

In Barbados, where rum is cheaper than bottled water, locals drink it with fresh green coconut water, hacking a hole in the green coconut and pouring a drop in. At home, try mixing rum with a drop of fresh coconut water, but watch the calories. Or, as fresh coconuts can be harder to come by once you move out of the Caribbean, Jules Gauldoni has also developed this watermelon version for a party drink.

RUM WATERMELON

1. Take a big, juicy watermelon and bore two one-inch-diameter holes two inches apart.

2. Turn the watermelon upside down in the sink and allow the juices to drain for a couple of hours.

3. Once drained, place an open bottle of aged blanco rum upside down in one of the holes and allow the watermelon to get drunk for twenty-four hours.

4. Refrigerate, and then take your drunken watermelon for a picnic with some friends. (If you keep hold of the juices, you can also serve this up in a bowl as a melon fruit punch.)

RUM-BLES OF DANGER ON MOJITOS

The divine Alan Carr was in celebratory mood when we met for lunch at the Ivy. He had just signed a contract for his new series with Channel 4. This called for a cocktail, and Mojitos were just the ticket.

We spent an idyllic lunch in a beautiful whirl chatting and chortling.

The sun was shining and we were in proper trim and ready to carry on. Arm in arm we strolled joyfully through

Soho, our laughter booming up and down Old Compton St.

Alan said that he knew a jolly place where we could have a drink, sit outside and watch the goings-on at the brothel at the end of the road. An idea that, on the outside of a Mojito, seemed strangely delightful!

We arranged a table outside the bar with a perfect vantage point. A girl appeared in the doorway of the brothel, which was about twenty metres away. We both realised that she looked like someone.

Excitedly, and in a pitch and volume that can only be described as the farthest thing away from a whisper, Alan cried out, 'It's Britney Spears! She's a bit scabby but it is Britney, loooook!!!' He was right – there was really quite a good resemblance.

About ten minutes passed and 'Britney' went back inside and then another girl came out to stand in the brothel doorway. Together Alan and I both shrieked, 'Beyonce!' She was indeed a very convincing looky-likey.

In the next thirty minutes we saw a Scarlett Johansson, a Naomi Campbell and a J-Lo. It was truly an Oscar-winning line-up.

None of the girls looked happy at all. Alan and I watched with intense curiosity. From twenty metres away they all looked just like the real stars. Thankfully we were not in Beverly Hills, otherwise Alan may have felt the urge to rush over to invite them to appear on his show.

After another round of cocktails, we had it all worked out and were totally convinced that these girls were being held by sex traffickers and needed rescuing. We'd both seen a documentary about this very thing and decided we'd go and rescue them all.

Alan elected that I should be the one to enter the brothel as I would blend in more easily . . . hmmmmm!!!

As 'Britney' came out for her second doorway rotation we felt the time was right for me to make my move. There was a window at the very top of the building and I needed to make it up to that window and work my way down, letting the girls know that they were being taken to safety.

Alan made me promise that once I reached that window I was to open it and wave down at him to let him know that I was all right. He said that if I didn't wave within ten minutes he'd know that I was in trouble and he'd come in and get me. It was all becoming so fabulously James Bondular.

I walked over to 'Britney'. With every step I took she seemed to age. It was like watching one of those nature programmes showing the life of a rose in five seconds. Bud, bloom, wilt, compost. She had reached the mid-point of wilt.

I introduced myself but she didn't speak any English. As luck would have it, Beyonce turned up at this point and like a game of charades I started to mime that I was there to rescue them. Beyonce also looked confused. I went in and made my way up the stairs.

As I raced up to the top window, I passed a man on the stairs leaving a room and saying goodbye to J-Lo. I finally made it to the top floor and knocked on the door. A very pleasant and rather surprised Russian girl opened the door and let me in. Her room was very neat, with red walls, black furnishings and white sheep-pelt rugs. Just how I would imagine the decor would be in the Cheeky Girls' house.

I went over to the window and opened it to wave my secret signal to Alan only to find a huge crowd looking up at me and cheering loudly. Alan had told everyone. The man who was with J-Lo was quite bewildered and astonished as he emerged from the brothel to see a cheering crowd and Alan roaring encouragement, waving a Mojito and bellowing, 'Well done, Cleo.'

I shot back in before being found out. I moved quickly to round up the girls and told them that they must go to the bar across the road where they could have a drink and we'd help them escape.

Though none of them spoke much English, they did seem to understand the bit about going across the road for a drink.

The rescue mission was in full swing. As I approached the bottom of the stairs, I heard a man's voice. He sounded

distinctly cross. I stopped in my tracks as I heard him
come closer. I hid around the corner and as he passed,
I managed to catch a glimpse of him. He was a large
foreboding figure wearing a pair of jodhpurs and a wacky
country-style outfit with a riding crop and topped off with
an eccentric hat.

I dashed out of the brothel. Alan and the crowd
were proudly cheering, their glasses raised. Alan had
already bought the girls some drinks and was hiding
them in the centre of the crowd. We finally managed to
make them understand that we wanted to help them to
escape. They looked stunned and started to laugh. To our
total shock none of them wanted to leave. Apparently
they were all very happy working there and being well
treated.

The crowd parted, the ground shook and once again
I heard that booming angry voice. It was the pimp
striding towards us, cutting the air with his riding crop.
He stood haughtily, with his hands on his hips and
loomed menacingly, casting a huge cold shadow over us.
'So what's this? What are you doing with my girls?' he
demanded. There was complete silence in the bar. Alan
and I were rigid with fear. There was a long pause. He let
out a terrifying laugh, which was the last thing that we
expected, and roared in a heavy Eastern European accent,
'I am extremely thirsty.' He sat down at our table, shifting

his noticeable buttocks from cheek to cheek as if trying to dislodge a wedgie.

'The good news for you both, my dear friends,' he said, waving his riding crop under our noses, 'is that after a few drinks I become a pooooooossycat, a very, very FORGIVING poooooossycat.'

Alan and I gulped anxiously. 'Mojitos it is, then, and keep them coming, bartender,' we cried!

HOW TO MAKE THE PERFECT MOJITO TO APPEASE AN ANGRY PIMP

35ml anejo blanco rum
25ml fresh lime juice or juice of one lime
20ml AquaRiva organic agave syrup
25ml good quality club soda
A handful of fresh mint including the stalks, to be
crushed in shaker glass with the agave syrup
Lots of crushed ice

Gently shake and pour into a long glass. Garnish with fresh mint.

A QUICK POSITIVE DRINKING QUIZ ON RUM

So it's the morning after? How's your head?

☐ A little fuzzy, but I'll live. Ah well done, you diligently took the anejo blanco route, drank it long with a natural sugar-free mixer and you danced and laughed, I take it?

☐ Oh God. I appear to be on a boat with the undead. Ah, good evening. Was it Captain Jack? Listen, have you ever thought of just switching your tipple to 100 per cent agave tequila ?

'If you keep on drinking rum, the world will soon be quit of a very dirty scoundrel.'
Robert Louis Stevenson

OH, I DON'T KNOW – THERE'S WORSE STUFF OUT THERE. LIKE BLUE CURACAO.

LESSON TEN

THE CRAIC ABOUT BLUE CURACAO

Blue Curacao is utterly brilliant at removing mildew.

But I really don't recommend that you drink it.

LESSON ELEVEN

THE PERILS OF PARTY PLANNING

Of course, I know you're fabulous and will have been invited to every party in town. But do not fear if you do not have an invitation to a party that you particularly wish to attend. There are several ways to disguise yourself in order to gain entry to even the most exclusive of dos. For the first I shall employ a disguise technique that has been successfully used by world leaders: a uniform.

DRINKING WITH WORLD LEADERS – A GUIDE TO DRINKING DISGUISES

A superb way to get yourself into a private members' establishment or party that for some reason you're not invited to (don't they know how fabulous you are?) is to wear something that vaguely looks like a uniform. People go blind when faced with uniforms. Once they're on, people tend not to look the person in the face, they just see the uniform. I can throw in a couple of world leaders to illustrate this point if it helps.

Benazir Bhutto was a chum and had once driven me to a Cost Cutter in Edgware Road, declaring that she'd run out of her favourite ingredient, tinned tomatoes. Bhutto, the revered former prime minister of Pakistan and one of the most extraordinary women in history, was wearing her head scarf. As we chatted our way towards the canned goods, one young man, seeing the head covering, which was similar to that worn by the store's staff, asked Benazir where the wine was kept. She happily directed him, and the woman who was an inspiration to billions and icon of Pakistan even added in a few recommendations for drinks without him ever twigging who she was. She was in possession of the most mischievous sense of humour.

And I heard a glorious tale once about Nelson Mandela, in which he was a guest and also in hiding at a rather grand house in South Africa many decades ago. On this particular evening the owners of the house were throwing an elegant dinner party for Mandela and their society guests. The owners received word that armed police were on their way up the long drive with the intention of searching the house, as they were on the hunt for Mandela. In a moment of sheer ingenuity the hosts thrust Mandela into a waiter's uniform and hurriedly escorted him into the kitchen where he was to stay with the other staff. The hosts greeted the Chief of Police warmly and exchanged polite banter while the house was thoroughly searched. To the amazement of the hosts and dinner guests, Mandela appeared in the room with a tray of sherry and offered the Chief of Police a glass. He did not recognise Mandela. He saw him purely as a faceless member of staff, never looked him in the eye, drank his sherry and was on his way.

Lord Lucan is probably buttling somewhere now. As long as he is in uniform no one would ever know.

Mind you, I too have been guilty of just seeing the uniform. There was once an occasion in Number 10 with Kenny Everett. Having settled comfortably with a glass of champagne on one of the few sofas available in the crowded room, it became apparent that the drinks were more than a little on the slow side. A woman wearing what looked like waitress's attire was walking past and Kenny tried to attract her attention with: 'waitress, waitress' before tugging at this woman's arm. She turned round. It was Margaret Thatcher. He did apologise profusely. However, the lady was not for turning again and she didn't go and get us a drink.

Anyway, all this posing as staff by world leaders can be adapted by those without countries to run in order to improve the status and venues of their cocktail experiences.

A handy accessory when attempting to drink in a crowded place with a huge queue to the bar and no VIP pass is one of those bright yellow or green tabards with glow-in-the-dark strips that security people wear. They also come in incredibly handy when boarding a crowded train to events such as Epsom or Ascot if one is to arrive before the champagne gets warm. Simply pop the jacket on over your clothes, shout: 'Back, everyone! OK! Crew, come through now please! Everyone else back! All these people need to come through.' You then simply gather and proceed to lead your friends calmly to the front. A friend perfected this technique with great style at a train station when urgently needing to board a train to Epsom to catch his race in time. A whistle or a walkie-talkie can add to the look.

Reporters at the notorious *News of the World* used the uniform trick all the time when working undercover. A favourite trick was to blag their way into celebrity weddings and parties wearing a black-tie waiter or waitress outfit, carrying a tray of champagne. Guests would rush towards the free drinks and the uniformed reporters would say that they were off to the kitchen for more champagne and would then waltz straight into the party.

Alternatively, for the daring who want to attend awards ceremonies or parties without a ticket, simply purchase a stethoscope and a first-aid kit and march past security and into the room declaring: 'OK, where's the patient?'

I once spent a flight home from South Africa with Alan Carr in which we became a little bored, so to liven things up a bit, I popped open a cupboard in the first class cabin where a staff uniform was hanging. On went the jacket, the scarf and the hat and I then wandered down the aisle taking drinks orders.

Thankfully I went to drama school and have a pretty good memory for scripts so the drinks orders were remembered and fulfilled and the cabin was well refreshed in no time. Funnily enough, not one person looked me in the face or recognised that I was the same person they had just been merrily chatting to minutes earlier. They all spoke to the uniform, ignored the face and just carried on with their drinks requests.

If it's your own party, then obviously keep an eye on which scoundrels in uniform are interloping their way in.

'At every party there are two kinds of people – those who want to go home and those who don't. The trouble is, they are usually married to each other.'
American advice columnist Ann Landers

Here, to help things go with a swing, are some perfect cocktails and the amounts you'll need for catering for multiple guests. They're the recipes I use when throwing parties for my guests, which include

Holly Willoughby, Keith Lemon, Derren Brown, Kelly Brook and the entire cast of *Dallas*. I'm happy to report everyone emerged hangover-free the next day.

I've given quantities for fifty guests, with three cocktails assumed for each guest.

NO-HANGOVER MOJITO FOR FIFTY GUESTS

8 bottles of Reposado or Anejo 100 per cent agave tequila
150 fresh limes or 3750ml of fresh lime juice
12 250ml bottles of organic agave syrup
6 bottles of a good quality club soda
Several large bunches of fresh mint

Each drink should contain 35ml tequila, the juice of one lime
(or 25ml), 20ml organic agave syrup and 25ml of a good quality
club soda. Gently shake and pour into a large glass and garnish
with fresh mint.

NO-HANGOVER GUAVARITA FOR FIFTY GUESTS

8 bottles of 100 per cent agave Blanco or Reposado tequila
150 fresh limes
750ml of guava purée or 1.25 litres of guava juice
12 250ml bottles of organic agave syrup

Each drink should contain 35ml tequila, juice of one lime,
15ml guava purée or 25ml guava juice.

MEXICAN 55 FOR FIFTY GUESTS

5 bottles of champagne or prosecco
6 bottles of 100 per cent agave blanco tequila
12 250ml bottles of organic agave syrup
90 fresh limes or 1350ml fresh lime/lemon juice
1 bottle of grapefruit bitters

Each drink should contain 35ml tequila, 15ml fresh squeezed
lemon juice, 15ml agave syrup, 2 dashes of grapefruit bitters.
Shake all ingredients except the champagne over ice and serve in a
champagne flute. Top up each glass at the last moment as guests
arrive with a splash of champagne or prosecco, so you keep the fizz
as fresh as possible.

ELDERFLOWER, SKINNY TEQUILA AND CHAMPAGNE COCKTAIL FOR FIFTY GUESTS

Follow the recipe on page 54, halving the quantities.

At every party, as well as water, you should provide a non-alcoholic
cocktail to encourage your guests to have a little break between
rounds. Always have well-presented and stylish jugs of water to hand
to encourage your guests to keep properly hydrated

On page 201 you'll find a recipe for a fake pink gin, which does the
trick perfectly. It will also allow drivers and other non-drinkers to feel

part of the party, without bloating up on sugar and chemicals from cola, or getting increasingly acidic and uncomfortable after litres of fruit juice.

LET'S GET THE PARTY STARTED

FAQ: Can you recommend any special equipment I should buy when holding a drinks party? Something to impress my guests?

As explained before, you don't need fancy cocktail making equipment. A Tupperware container with a lid makes a perfectly good shaker. You don't need expensive glasses – just hire them from an off-licence. But it is, if possible, a good idea to install a hedge.

Yes. A hedge. Let me explain.

THE MODESTY HEDGE

If you're holding an event with a top table at which there will be ladies present I would urge you to install a Modesty Hedge. You'll thank me when you get your photos back.

You will notice that at all high-society functions such as polo or elegant garden parties that wherever seating is provided for ladies settling down for a long and jolly lunch, the table will have a strategically placed short hedge in front of it. Failing that it will have a long table cloth.

This is a Modesty Hedge. It means that ladies sitting on the top table who have a drop too much to drink and perhaps forget to sit with their knees quite as together as they should, as a result, are not flashing their most intimate garments to all and sundry.

This technique goes back to the olden days. Look at old portraits of lively dinners and you will see tapestries, tablecloths, shrubs or small cherubs hanging about in front of tables neatly shielding the viewer's eye from anything untoward. Visit a couple of art galleries and you will see what I mean. Look at Leonardo da Vinci's *Last Supper* for example: a nice long tablecloth. No matter what betrayal was going on around the table, all participants could rest assured that a nice neat length of tablecloth was included which fell below the knee, ensuring full modesty for all.

Do remember this tip if holding a wedding or drinks reception in your garden. That way the ladies can recline, relax and enjoy the refreshments, secure in the knowledge that when the photos come out none of them are showing their 'knickers'.

Incidentally, talking of 'knickers', as well as a well-stocked drinks cabinet and a return to graceful drinking, please may I again make an impassioned plea for a return to graceful dressing too.

> *'I dress to kill, but tastefully.'*
> **Freddie Mercury**

LESSON TWELVE

HOW TO REMAIN FRESH ON A PLANE

'There is an art . . . to flying. The knack lies in learning how to throw yourself at the ground and miss.'
Douglas Adams, *The Hitchhikers Guide to the Galaxy*

'And to maybe throw yourself away from the bar and miss that sometimes too. Let me explain the art of drinking on planes.'
Cleo Rocos

Well, I think you know by now that I am all for having a good time and on occasion I have even been known to throw my last scruple happily to the wind. But when it comes to aeroplanes, I'd advise a little more caution and a little less alcohol.

I like to view an aeroplane as a magnificent winged vessel cleverly designed to transport you to your next exciting cocktail destination. Not a flying bar. Let me explain, as I do hate to sound like a killjoy.

Hopefully you are boarding a plane to arrive somewhere wonderful and not being deported or heading anywhere without proper facilities, in which case aeroplanes are key in enabling you to magically cross time zones, mountains and seas and get you to those hard-earned holiday cocktails. (If you're on one for something dreadful or going to see someone you really can't bear, then forget all the following, good luck and ask for a large one ASAP.)

The trick with planes is to stay as fresh and fragrant as possible in-flight so you can take full advantage of the delights that the bartender will be creating when you arrive at your enchanting destination. One does not wish to arrive hot, bloated, desperate for sleep, and already hungover from guzzling cheap alcohol whilst strapped into a seat in a metal, cylindrical shed suspended a mile up in the air.

All of which is easier said than done.

It's so tempting to drink on planes, isn't it? The second one steps on board someone's there with a lovely smile and a crisp uniform, offering you a drink. And inside it's all a bit like Vegas – there are no clocks on the aeroplane walls so everything's permanently set to cocktail time. Even if it's 9 o' clock in the morning, those beautiful people in airline uniforms are gliding up and down the aisle assuring you that it's *absolutely entirely normal* to have a tipple at this time.

But stop and think before you reach for that drink.

Tread carefully in your Mile High bar or you'll be landing at your destination with a jumbo jet of a hangover. Some rules apply if you wish to drink positively.

It's time for another FAQ. And some maths.

FAQ: Why do I seem to get so drunk, so quickly, on planes?

'Newton's Law states that what goes up, must come down.
Our Company Commander's Law states that what
goes up and comes down had damn well better be
able to go back up again.'

Sign in the Operations Office of the 187th Assault
Helicopter Company, Tay Ninh, Vietnam, 1971.

'Unless it comes to your inflight drinks. Follow these rules of
drinking and your tipple will slip down without mishap.'
Cleo Rocos

Drinking mid-air is fraught with hazards. The old adage that one drink in the air feels like three on the ground is correct.

THE SCIENCE BIT

Back to our scientifically minded drinking companion Dr Bull who has been kind enough to research this for me and says: 'When you drink alcohol on a plane, it does **not** make your blood alcohol level increase any higher than drinking on the ground.

'BUT it's thought you feel more drunk because the lower partial pressure of oxygen means that you have less oxygen in your blood, which means less is getting to your brain, so the feeling of drunkenness occurs more markedly.'

On top of that, other factors come into play. Firstly people rarely eat before they get on a plane. So they tend to be drinking on an empty stomach, meaning the alcohol is absorbed more rapidly.

They also tend to drink faster than usual. As Dr Bull points out: 'This means the blood alcohol content rises very quickly giving the feeling of intoxication.'

Thirdly they're also often exhausted having got up early and raced to the airport to catch the flight.

All these factors combined mean that each sip you have on board is three for the price of one on your brain. Not realising this can get you into some unforeseen and dreadful situations. It once led to a very hairy flight where a TV star friend of mine almost got arrested. More of that later.

So make sure you eat before you get on the plane, or at least have a glass of milk to slow things down. Don't automatically go for early-morning flights either, I've got a guide to the perfect flying times to arrive in time for cocktails around the world coming up in a minute.

And take things easy. Remember that drinking-wise, you're already halfway there, so rather than hard-core spirits go for longer cocktails, less strong ABV drinks, and only drink when you eat your meal to avoid landing with a raging hangover after just a couple of glasses.

Over-refreshed or worse drunkenness is not the only pitfall of inflight drinking. Let's look at some other easily avoidable problems.

UNWANTED EMISSIONS

Drink the wrong thing and your insides can start creating their own personal air turbulence and if you're not careful you may be doing a little jet propulsion of your own.

This is not good manners.

Just because it's an aeroplane, please do not feel it acceptable to contribute to the cabin pressure. Any propulsions you make will ripple through the aircraft and sit there for the duration of the flight.

Incidentally, one poor passenger found this out to her cost during a 2006 American Airlines flight. The flight was forced into an emergency landing after passengers reported the smell of burned matches. A female passenger later admitted she'd struck the match in an effort to conceal a little fumey turbulence around her seat. Sadly she only admitted it after being singled out by a series of bomb-sniffing dogs, which tracked the scent right to her seat.

So, to avoid bomb-sniffing dogs, avoid the following:

Bubbles This is the number-one rule. Say no to champagne, sodas, tonics, beers, or any fizzy drinks. None of these are going to help the situation. Those bubbles go in and they've got to come out somewhere. So curb your desire to no more than a glass or it will backfire on both you and your fellow passengers with no good results at all.

Say no to the pretzels and bread rolls The wheat won't help matters of personal turbulence either.

Dress Codes for Drinking You should also avoid any tight clothing. Your Hervé Léger dress or corset may look stylish but those very close-fitting garments will do you no favours on an aeroplane. This is why all the passengers in First Class are given a nice pair of comfy pyjamas to wear as they board. It's so that they can eat, drink and rest without any issues, then pop on their restrictive foundation garments and an outfit upon arrival and still look catwalk fresh for the photographers.

The good news is that you can still drink and avoid all this – in fact a Bloody Mary can help if one adds a little black pepper; it'll help calm everything down. Just stick to one, though, as they can be packed with salt, which can lead to bloating and cankles (see later). If any food is offered with ginger try this as it can also help calm things down. Packing a sushi takeaway lunch from the airport and eating this on board is always a wise and healthier option and can help nip things in the bud before your bud nips you.

If you're struck then keep close to the facilities and try to keep all objectionable expulsions safely in there.

FAQ: How much should I drink on a plane?

The correct answer is not as many alcoholic beverages as they will give you.

As with much in life, it's all a question of timing. A lot depends on whether your destination is ahead or behind in timelines. If you're going to somewhere that's five hours ahead and you're going to land in the dead of night when everything's shut and all you can do is sleep then it seems a shame not to take some advantage of the complimentary bar on board. But if you're going to somewhere that's behind in time and will be arriving just in time for pre-dinner cocktails, then it makes no sense to arrive six sheets to the wind and having to miss a lovely evening and cocktail experience.

There's a science to it:

$$\text{How many G\&T} = ZxY/X$$

Z is what time you are arriving and X is what time you board the plane; Y is the amount of cocktail appreciation hours you will have at your destination and a nice G&T is what you should be working out if you should be saying yes or no to.

Confused? Here's how to work it out:

On boarding a plane immediately set your watch to local time at your destination. Then work out what time you will be having your first cocktail on land and how long the bar is open after you arrive.

Adjust all cocktail quantities according to this data.

Let's try some examples.

Say you're on a 2 p.m. flight from London to New York's JFK Airport.

How lovely. The chocolate Martinis are heaven out there.

Back to your flight, it's 2 p.m. back home, but what time is it in the cocktail venues to which you're flying? In this example (in British Summer Time), New York is five hours behind London. It's 9 a.m.

Now, let's look at the cocktail situation when you land. It's about a 7–8 hour flight so let's say ETA is about 4.30 p.m. That means you'll be through customs, into a yellow cab and, with good traffic and good service in Manhattan by early evening. All the best bars and restaurants are still open for a good five or six hours so plenty of time for cocktails.

You do not want to waste this.

Don't think that you're getting on a flight at 2 p.m., you're on holiday, and therefore you have earned a drink. Think instead that it's 9 a.m. in the morning and in ten hours' time you'll be going out for drinks. Throttle back. Say no. Just because you are in the air and someone's offering it you're not actually legally obliged to drink it. Save yourself. Do not drink on this flight. Well, maybe one at lunch, but that's it. Keep yourself radiant and in proper trim for later.

Don't worry, it isn't always the case where I suggest that you turn down complimentary alcoholic refreshments. I just want you to have the most enjoyable time on your travels. Let's try another flight. Your return flight. Only this time, you are travelling to somewhere that's ahead of you in time.

Your flight leaves New York at 11 a.m., arriving in London at 11 p.m.

Let's set our watches first. It's 11 a.m. in New York but 3 p.m. in London. Next, let's look at arrival time. 11 p.m. in London. So, by the time you've got your suitcases and have braved the motorways, you're unlikely to hit Central London before midnight. Cocktail time at your destination is severely limited. Under the rules of the yard arm (see page 2), it's perfectly acceptable to have a drink whenever you like as technically it's been past noon for three hours since you stepped on board. **In this instance I would consider throwing my FAQs out the window and treating myself to exactly what I desired. That's if there's nothing waiting for you at the other end but a good sleep.**

A GUIDE TO THE IDEAL FLYING TIMES

Instead of getting an early-morning flight and racing to the airport on lack of sleep and lack of breakfast, why not plan your trips so that you always arrive in time for pre-dinner cocktails and can get over your journey with a glorious evening?

Don't worry. I've done all the maths for you. Here are some suggested flight times that I prepared for you earlier. All will get you to your arrival destination by early afternoon, therefore allowing an hour or two for transfers, faffing about with suitcases, all topped off with a much-anticipated chilled cocktail to be served before it's time for dinner.

(All are in British Summer Time, which is the last Sunday of March to the last Sunday of October.) Outside that you may wish to knock back an hour to avoid disappointment.

ATHENS (two hours ahead, flight: three hours forty mins) A 10.40 a.m. flight will land you late afternoon and be about right. Have a post-lunch drink on board, they don't mind. The Greeks like wine so much they invented a God for it – Dionysos.

AZERBAIJAN (four hours ahead, flight: five hours thirty mins) Is that where you're off to? Well, I'm glad someone was paying attention to all those Eurovision videos. A 5 a.m. flight will land you there late afternoon and you will find the Azeri wine is more than enjoyable.

BALI (seven hours ahead, flight: sixteen–nineteen hours) You'll probably have to change flights and will arrive a day after you set off. No one expects you to refuse the joys on offer from the cocktail trolley, so get on an evening flight from London and ask for a Bloody Mary immediately.

BARBADOS – Bridgetown (five hours behind, flight: eight hours forty mins) An 11.20 a.m. flight will have you there for about 3 p.m., enabling a quick transfer and the chance of a Mount Gay rum cocktail in the Lonestar before dinner. For supper I recommend an ocean seat at The Cliff.

BENIDORM – Alicante (one hour ahead, flight: two hours thirty mins). A noon flight will have you there for around 3.30 p.m. Fly whatever time you like though – they'll already all be well over-refreshed. I would recommend one or two on board. They've been on happy hour for years now and rumour has it that you'll need a stiff one before taking in some of the local cabaret.

DUBAI (three hours ahead, flight: seven hours) Hmmm, it's not really a drinker's paradise out there. It's a minefield of drinking laws. Get an early morning flight – 6 or 7 a.m. to arrive early evening. And don't even think about drinking on the plane. Drunk and disorderly through customs is not a good look and rightly not tolerated at all.

FIJI (eleven hours ahead, flight: twelve hours) So set off in the early evening, and do not drink if you're on a morning flight. Arriving over-refreshed at breakfast is not acceptable, classy or stylish.

ITALY – Rome (one hour ahead, flight: two hours thirty mins) Travel around lunchtime. No real need to imbibe on the flight. You are going to the home of fine wines after all.

JAMAICA (six hours behind, flight: ten hours) Go for a noon flight, which will get you into Montego Bay for about 4 p.m. and through customs in time to see the sunset over a cocktail at Rick's Café.

LOS ANGELES (eight hours behind, flight: eleven hours) LA shuts horribly early as everyone gets up and jogs in the morning. So I'd get there early. In this case take a flight at about noon and it will get you there for about 3 p.m.

MEXICO (six hours behind, flight: ten hours twenty mins) A noon flight will set you down nicely in Cancun at around 4 p.m. ensuring a tequila cocktail or two before dinner. If you are lucky enough to be flying upper class Virgin Atlantic they have Clubhouses in Heathrow and Gatwick. Ask for no-hangover Margaritas and Guavaritas – my best cocktail experience in the air with absolutely zero nasty effects, and one is fresh to continue once arrived.

MOSCOW (three hours ahead, flight: three hours fifty-five minutes) A 9 a.m. flight will ensure you're there for about 4 p.m. You'll be encouraged to consume your body weight in vodka when you land so I'd throttle back on the Martinis en route.

PARIS (one hour ahead, flight: one hour twenty mins) Set off around 2 p.m. and you will be sipping along the Seine by early evening. But frankly, why on earth are you flying? Get the Eurostar! That way you can bring more of France's finest wines home. Set off at breakfast and be there for a late lunch.

REHAB CLINIC IN ARIZONA (seven hours behind, flight: eleven hours twenty mins) Good luck. It's said to be the sternest in the world. No pre-dinner drinks for you when you get there so set off whenever. I'd say get on there early and you may as well have one for the road.

SPAIN – Madrid (one hour ahead, flight: two hours thirty mins) A 1 p.m. flight will have you there at 4 p.m., well settled and ready for your first Rioja of the evening.

ST LUCIA (four hours behind, flight: eight hours) Go for a noon flight, you will land in plenty of time for pre-dinner Bounty rum cocktails between the Pitons.

SYDNEY (nine hours ahead, flight: twenty-two hours) There's no easy way of doing this journey as you're stuck on that plane for the next twenty-four hours, facing a stopover, and day is night when you get there so you'll feel hellish for the next few days anyway. Personally, I'd say just get on and have a drink. Work things out when you get there. To stand the best chance of spending as much of the flight as possible in a happy slumber, I'd board about 10 p.m. London time, and take a sleeping pill. I always enjoy the soporific effects of a Dramamine motion-sickness pill with half a glass of wine. It knocks me out within half an hour. If needs must you are then free to take the precaution of having a few cocktails during your stopover in Hong Kong and you should arrive two days later at 6 a.m., when it is perfectly acceptable to go back to bed for another nap and arise in the late afternoon.

UTAH (six hours behind, around an eleven-hour flight with a changeover) Why are you going there? The liquor laws are still a nightmare. Frankly, my advice is to arrive at your departure airport early, go straight to the Duty Free and stock up before you get on board. Then have a good old go at sampling the wares on the trolley during the flight, for safe measure.

SEATING ARRANGEMENTS FOR DRINKERS ON FLIGHTS

If you're not intending to drink or eat on a flight then ask for a window seat, and you can relax, sleep or enjoy the view without interruption from either the stewards with the trolleys or your fellow passengers asking you to get up whenever they need to excuse themselves.

If you're intending to have a glass or two, I'd go for an aisle seat so you can have a good long drink of water to counteract dehydration effects and easily get in and out of your seat without annoying everyone. If you're on an aisle seat planning a teetotal session and you spot the person in the window seat going hell for leather with the champagne, ask if they'd like to swap seats as they'll spend the entire flight clambering all over you otherwise.

Emergency exit seats are completely worth the £50 or so extra they cost – just so you can jump up freely and without disturbing anyone or being disturbed yourself.

Of course, if you're in First Class and flat out in your own private bed, then lucky you. Don't worry about your rehydration attempts interrupting anyone else's flight. Have you noticed first-class passengers just look brighter, fresher and more radiant at the other end? That's because they can all knock back an ocean of water without having to queue for the loo, can sleep restfully with a blanket and flat bed and arrive perfectly fresh at their destination ready to party.

UPGRADES

Talking of First Class, do everything you can to get an upgrade. Everything's so much better in First Class. It's so much easier to drink positively in there as everything is of a much better quality. It's easier to maintain everything.

Ask politely for an upgrade. There's no harm in it. Often seats are oversold in economy but there's room in Business or First. Dress with style and panache, as if you belong in First, and be gracious to the flight attendants as you board. Don't go over the top, though, and start murmuring to the Captain: 'Shall we make Budapest a stopover to remember?' Just smile and be your wonderful polite self.

If you get upgraded you may like to show your appreciation to the flight attendants who arranged your upgrade with gifts of perfume to say thank you. You may end up with the same crew on the return journey and it does no harm for word of your largesse and appreciation to be known.

FAQ: Why do so many people order Bloody Marys on planes?

One survey compiled for a holiday site found that nearly a quarter of flyers ordered a Bloody Mary on a flight but never drank them at any other time. For some reason, it tasted amazing in-flight but the same drink tasted earthy, musty and salt-laden on the ground.

The reason for this is that ingredients will taste different at different altitudes. The reduced pressure in the plane cabin deadens your taste buds by as much as 30 per cent for both salt and sugar. Taste-wise it's roughly the same as eating when you've got a streaming cold. So a tomato juice that may taste musty on ground level suddenly becomes fruity and sweet on a plane, no matter how much salt has been ladelled in there.

Equally suddenly those salty pretzel and peanut snacks seem utterly irresistible, and you tuck into biscuits, cakes, bread and salt- and sugar- filled snacks with abandon.

All of which, I'm afraid, leads to those cankles.

A whole heap of salt intake leads to a whole heap of bloating, which then takes at least two days to go down from the feet up.

HOW TO MAKE A LOW-SALT BLOODY MARY

(Drink on the way to the airport. If you're not driving, obviously.)

100ml low-sodium V8 vegetable juice
35ml Absolut Pepper Vodka
juice of half a lime
four dashes Lea and Perrins
20ml dry sherry
half tsp English mustard
two dashes Tabasco Pepper sauce

Add the ingredients to your airline glass and stir.

FAQ: So, what should I drink on a plane?

Having established that the correct answer is not always to consume as many alcoholic beverages as they will give you, what should we order from that trolley?

To keep ankles slim, restrict yourself to just one drink, or one bottle of wine with dinner. That's an airliner-size mini bottle of wine by the way – i.e., one wine glass – not a full-sized bottle. Wine can also contain histamines, which add to this swelling effect, and any more than a glass can send your blood sugar levels shooting all over the place meaning you fall upon anything parading as food that passes under your nose.

If available, my 100 per cent agave tequila Margarita cocktail is again an excellent choice as it contains natural anti-histamines, and acid flavours like fresh lime still taste the same in the pressurised environment. The organic agave syrup is much sweeter than sugar, which helps you taste it and keep your GI levels stable as well as being gluten free. It will not induce sudden hunger or ridiculous food cravings either. Organic agave syrup is an appetite suppressant.

Even if that Bloody Mary tastes terrific, check the labels for sodium levels, as these can be up to 27 per cent in some tomato drinks. Flavour your drink with pepper instead of salt and hold back on the Worcestershire sauce as it's flavoured with anchovies and high in salt. Refuse those salted peanuts and pretzels that come round with the drinks. If you're lucky enough to have turned left and are in First Class you can footle about asking questions regarding low-salt choices, but if you're stuck in economy do make arrangements in advance to protect your cankles. Order low-sodium meals if the airline gives a choice, or shop in the airport shops for desirable and fresh food and take your own healthy feast on board. If you're having just one drink, then it may be better to have one just before boarding the flight and stick to water whilst flying. That way you are not automatically consuming high levels of salt and sugar to get the taste, and you will board feeling pleasantly relaxed.

A gin and tonic is a good choice, too, as the gin contains juniper berries, which helps with kidney functions to guard against swelling, but stick to just one or the bubbles in the tonic will work against you.

Eating before you board is a good rule, too. If I can avoid it I never eat on board at all. For short-haul flights I just get to the airport early, have a wonderful relaxed meal there and have nothing but water on the flight. It won't kill you to miss a meal for a few hours and it frees you up to go to sleep because you don't have to wait for the trolley coming round. Best of all you'll arrive with enviable ankles and an appetite to enjoy a proper feast at your new destination.

For all the reasons above, I think that private jets are often a waste of money. So many private jet terminals are just sheds with no shops, bars or restaurants to enjoy. They're completely boring. And on the flights the seats tend to face one another so unless you are just with your friends and people you adore, you have to engage with people when you may not feel like it and you simply can't relax.

Far better to go First Class on a commercial flight, get to the airport, have a premium quality drink, a lovely meal and then ponder around all the junk in Duty Free buying little things that you don't really need.

On the plus side private jets do have lovely padded lavatory seats.

HOW TO DRINK ON PLANES

If you're lucky enough to find yourself in a Virgin Atlantic Clubhouse Bar, then happily their bar staff are perfectly trained to make a Positive Margarita with my own AquaRiva Tequila to the instructions outlined in this book.

I was lucky enough to be on the inaugural flight to Mexico where I can confirm the magnificent bar staff served it solidly all the way there.

On arrival all the press, VIPs and celebrities were perfectly intact. In fact, Derren Brown got straight off the plane and did a pitch-perfect illusion show. Richard Branson held a wonderful presentation for the assembled press throng, and I went straight into the ocean in my cocktail gown.

EASY COCKTAILS TO MAKE FROM IN-PLANE INGREDIENTS

If you fly Virgin you can buy AquaRiva Reposado online duty free before your flight and that way you can enjoy and mix up my Positive Drinking tequila Margaritas on holiday (always drinking water during the flight too). Otherwise here is a list of common cocktails that you can mix at your seat using airplane ingredients.

Remember to take it easy, though. No more than two per flight, and, of course, only if you are not driving at the other end.

Bloody Mary: one airline vodka bottle, one tomato juice, pepper sachet from your lunch, one squeeze fresh lemon, dash Worcestershire sauce, touch of mustard.

Tom Collins Gin: one miniature bottle of gin, sugar (or preferably agave syrup), squeeze lemon juice, club soda, ice

Black Russian: vodka and Kahlua

White Russian: as above but add a splash of the milk served with your coffee.

Presbyterian: equal parts Scotch and ginger ale or 7-UP, splash club soda, ice

HOW NOT TO DRINK ON PLANES

A divine male A-list star had agreed to take part in my rather fabulous TV series that I was presenting and producing. We were heading off from Gatwick to film on location in the Caribbean. We had to fly firstly to Barbados where we would then catch a connecting flight to the beautiful and luscious island of Bequia where a large yacht with captain and crew would take us for a week of sailing around the islands in the Grenadines as we did our filming.

This was a hugely expensive trip, and I, as the executive producer, was in charge of the purse strings. In order to ensure the maximum possible amount of the budget was available for all incidentals, extras and the odd cocktail, it was decided that my male celebrity would turn left on the plane to First Class. The crew and I would turn right to steerage. My handsome friend, who was besieged by gleeful teenage girls and giggling hostesses upon boarding, merrily smiled and promised to send down some olives for us all.

What a glorious show this is going to be, I thought, whilst watching the grey skies of London evaporate into a bright sunshine that flooded the cabin with the heady notion of holiday happiness and delight. I went along to First Class to check on my star guest who seemed very comfortable and was contentedly sipping champagne. So I returned to my seat for lunch and to happily recline. We were, I thought, as I sipped an ice water and perused the film list, all on our wonderful way.

About five hours into the flight there was an announcement stating that all passengers must immediately return to their seats and fasten their seat belts. There was a hurricane up ahead coming straight for us. The pilot was, of course, going to do his best to avoid it but passengers were to remain seated at all times.

About an hour later the Chief Purser came over and politely gestured for me to remove my headphones. She looked distinctly uneasy as she whispered, 'We have a serious situation on our hands.' I was surprised and immediately thought the worst, wondering why she had chosen me to negotiate with the hijackers. She took me to one side and said, 'I have bad news for you. Several passengers in First Class are going to be arrested including your guest star.' I was absolutely astonished. This could not be happening!

Apparently one of the passengers in First Class had turned nasty and had become jealous after a few drinks. This passenger had insulted my guest star and had tried to punch him.

The main reason for the fight, it emerged, was that the aggressive passenger's wife, a Hobbit-like, stocky little arrangement with dangerously pendulous bosoms, had earlier happily asked my guest star for his autograph and had her photo taken with him. This he had agreed to and all was fine until she told her husband, by which time he was quite drunk and chose to react with abusive, out-of-control jealous rage.

It seems that she had also consumed several brandies and had now transformed into a boozy, violent street wench. Her husband was convinced the guest star was after his vile-mouthed woman and the pair shouted at passengers and my poor guest star, who at this point was being forced to fend off the aggressors. The plane's crew had to take appropriate measures, the police had been called, and the desperately unfair decision was made to arrest the lot of them upon landing.

One more thing, added the Chief Purser, none of them knew they were going to be arrested upon landing. And I was not permitted to tell my star as the Chief Purser felt it would make matters worse.

I was shocked into a state of calm. With an hour before landing my mind was racing. What was going to happen to my star? How was I going to get him out of this? All our filming plans. What about our programme? I sat quietly stunned and decided that I just had to come up with a solution. How do you explain to the Bajan police that just because a man is on the TV, it often causes

complete strangers to hurl abuse at him? He was going
to be held in a Bajan jail? How were we going to keep it
out of the press? Was it acceptable to offer the police a
charitable cash donation in a brown envelope and plead
for my friend to be released? What about the yacht and
my captain with a chef and a well-stocked bar waiting to
take us sailing around the Grenadines?

There was only one thing for it. My marvellous plan
was to carry on and film the show with or without my
guest star. We would film his interview in his cell – which
with clever lighting, some bright tropical plants in the
foreground, a giant poster of palm trees as a backdrop,
and a cocktail in his hand, could work. A little fake tan, a
straw hat and with a bit of computer wizardary, plus some
masterful sound edit of the sea, some gulls squawking and
boats, surely you'd barely see the joins?

My crew were all asleep. As the plane prepared to land I
told them about the problem up with our guest star in First
Class. They all went very quiet. I told them not to worry
and explained my plan. They were even quieter and now
very pale, too. Luckily at this point God clearly decided the
whole thing was desperately unfair, for we had a touch of
divine intervention. The plane lurched suddenly and then
dropped. Glasses fell off the tables and overhead lockers
popped opened. The pilot told us to stay in our seats as he
was trying to negotiate his way through the sudden and

fierce hurricane-related turbulence. We all sat there being violently rattled around from side to side and up and down.

After about fifteen minutes, the pilot announced that we were being diverted to Antigua as the hurricane was changing direction. And, miraculously, in the commotion to divert the plane away from the hurricane, it became clear that the pilot had forgotten to alert the police at the airport in Antigua.

We landed, no police were there, I saw my guest star up ahead walking calmly through the airport signing a few autographs and we rushed him into a cab to freedom.

I could see no reason why we should upset him and ruin a dream of a trip by telling him about the police. So we never told him at all. I asked how his flight had been, he said lovely, but for a couple of drunken idiots, and off we sped to the yacht. The filming, by the way, was an absolute triumph.

The moral of this story? Always stay sober on a flight. You can't rely on divine intervention to get you out of trouble, so stay divine and intervene yourself by staying sober so you can spot potential trouble and stay out of it.

I, of course, drank nothing of any interest during the entire flight, but trust me, the second I landed on the yacht we celebrated with some very large rum Daiquiris, or 'yacht-tails' as I like to call them, all round.

A RUM DAIQUIRI THAT'S PERFECT FOR WHEN YOU'VE JUST ESCAPED A JAIL SENTENCE

50ml blanco aged rum (I think you've earned a double)
15ml organic agave syrup
juice of one fresh squeezed lime

Shake over ice and serve, having first scanned the horizon for police.

'I don't like flying because I'm afraid of crashing into a large mountain. I don't think Dramamine is going to help.'
Kaffie, in the 1992 movie *A Few Good Men*

'I disagree. If my fellow passenger turns out to be less than exciting company I prescribe one large tequila or whisky and a dose of Dramamine and it'll be blissful oblivion til touchdown.'
Cleo Rocos

'In America there are two classes of travel – first class, and with children.'
Robert Benchley

And everywhere else. . . A resounding cheer to every airline that has banned children from their first-class compartments. Should you find yourself seated next to one on a flight and can't do anything about it, have a large one and take the Dramamine above.

Right, have we all landed safely? How about a celebratory chocolate?

LESSON TWELVE A

HOW TO REMAIN HOT WITH CHOCOLATE

'All you need is love. But a little chocolate now and then doesn't hurt.'
Charles M. Schulz

'Well, not quite right. There's no point drinking positively then diving into a chocolate hangover. Let's discover real chocolate that tastes exquisite and actually won't hurt you at all.'
Cleo Rocos

A positive-drinking experience is always accompanied by good food, which slows down alcohol absorption. But do be careful not to undo all your good work when it comes to the pudding stage. I wince at cocktail parties when canapés arrive serving cheap, sugar-loaded desserts. There's no point carefully making sugar-free drinks at a dinner party and then serving up a pudding which sends your guests spiraling into an ugly saccharine high.

I would suggest serving a simple, yet exquisite quality plain chocolate as a dessert, carefully matched to complement your drinks choices. Pairing chocolate with drinks is an interestingly different way to ignite your taste buds.

But just like alcohol, it's important to know the good and the bad of the chocolate world. So here is a lesson in real cocoa and what to buy. And specifically, how to deliver the ultimate mouth-marriage romance between a nibble of chocolate and a sip of drink.

Some chocolates are sweet, some bitter, some robust, some delicate. The trick is combining them with a perfect drinking partner to complement their characters and to result in the perfect marriage. It's nothing to do with cost, it's all about the particular cocoa bean from which the chocolate was made and the ingredients used to make your drink and ensuring you don't get an overload of sweetness or acidity.

We want layers of chocolately, alcohol joy as opposed to a combination that makes your teeth dry up so much you feel like you're chewing on a corrugated iron fence.

Think of me as a dating agency for your mouth.

FAQ: So, how do I choose a chocolate?

I'm going to quote my mother, who's in her eighties: when it comes to chocolate, once you've had black it's really hard to go back.

Pure dark chocolate really is the best for eating with alcohol. If you want to avoid the sugar high, avoid milk, avoid white chocolate at all costs, just buy the slabs of the purest dark chocolate available and combine this with your drink.

When it comes to choosing, your best bet is not to go for **brands** as an indicator of quality, but to look at the **ingredients list** on the label to see what's in there.

If it lists any of the following it is **Bad Chocolate**. No matter how seductively its label is murmuring that it's 'Belgian' or 'Luxury', put it back on the shelf and walk on:

NO:

Vegetable fat – or hydrogenated palm oil

'Flavourings' without saying what the flavourings are

Sugar – if listed as the first (i.e. main) ingredient.

Glucose syrup

Vanillan – (note the 'n' – vanilla extract is fine)

Vanilla 'essence' or 'flavouring' – again, extract is the word
 you want

Milk

Now, here are some indications that the bar you have in your hand will be good quality.

YES:

Cocoa Beans, listed **FIRST** in the list of ingredients. This can also be listed as 'cocoa mass', 'cocoa liquor' or 'cocoa solids'. If it's listed as the main ingredient, it's good stuff. You can pick that bad boy up now and sashay gleefully off to the till.

Sugar. It's fine for sugar to be present, as long as it's not the MAIN or first ingredient. The more you pay for your chocolate, the better quality this sugar is likely to be.

Cocoa butter – this is a natural fat and perfectly fine.

Vanilla extract

Sunflower or soya lecithin – again this is perfectly okay, it's a natural stabilizer. See that on the label and you're still good to go to the till.

No, actually the best chocolate bars readily available are usually the supermarket own labels. But go for the premium, not budget own-brand. They're every bit as good and often better than the branded bars.

MOUTH MARRIAGE

Right, let's get on with a drink, shall we? I'll do the types of drink, then suggest a compatible partner.

SWEET WHISKIES/BRANDIES/ARMAGNACS/ CHAMBORD/SWEET DESSERT WINES:

Ideal mouth-marriage match:

Madagascan dark chocolate (One that's around 64 per cent cocoa beans is fabulous)

Madagascan chocolate is fruity and acidic. The acidity creates water-falls in your mouth, as your tongue starts to water the second you nibble at it.

So you're looking for something with a more rounded and volup-tuous flavour, which is why these sweeter whiskies and bourbons, or a warming Armagnac are perfect. The sweet Chambord liqueur also works excellently, as the sweet raspberry combines well with the acidity.

What you must avoid is a Lily Savage of a concoction – anything acidic. Try it with anything like a limoncello, or a mandarin-flavoured vodka, and it will be like having blotting paper in your mouth and you may as well go and chew on some sawdust for all the pleasure you'll experience.

Very few wines work with this, other than perhaps a dessert wine with honey flavours.

MARTINIS/BLANCO TEQUILAS
Ideal mouth-marriage match:

Ecuadorian dark chocolate (I'd suggest something marked at 70 per cent)

A Tarzan of a taste, throbbingly botanical and floral from the jungle. But, on its own, it can be rather like eating a leathery loincloth, as it's so drying on the tongue. However, combine a nibble of this with a crisp Martini or fresh tequila and the dryness is softened, the flavour combination is naughtily seductive and leaves your mouth swooning. It's the Jane to the Tarzan in taste and the pair work superbly. Put the word out on the grapevine.

GRAPPA/EAU DE VIE/REPOSADO TEQUILAS/ STRONGER WHISKIES AND BRANDIES
Ideal mouth-marriage match:

100 per cent Ecuadorian dark chocolate

Give this sugar-free stick of dynamite of a chocolate a go. You can find the 100 per cent cocoa bars in specialist chocolate shops, and although it's not as widely available it's worth the search. On its own the 100 per cent cocoa bar is extremely drying in the mouth and almost alcoholic in taste, but pair it with a neat spirit and it just beautifully undresses around your taste buds. It's like eating your first day of a new romance.

Go for neat astringent spirits rather than cocktails. A whisky or a brandy combines wonderfully. Don't pair it with anything delicate in taste as it will just destroy it.

The advantage of this is that you and your guests will be sated after just one square of it, so skip making a dessert and just put down a square each with a digestif. It's a chic and divine sugar-free pudding. Of course, it would always be wise to have a little extra handy as the experience is so ravishing.

My mother's been on the pure dark chocolate for a few months now. She's lost half a stone and has never been so happy.

SHERRIES/PORT/DARK ROUNDED WHISKIES
Ideal mouth-marriage match:
Venezuelan dark chocolate.
Venezuelan dark chocolate on its own has a delicate, sweet flavour of toasted bread. (Look for one marked at around 72 per cent.)

Buy this one if you're planning to serve it with something stunningly robust. Rich sherries such as an Oloroso, a port with a decent left hook, or a dark rounded whisky.

CRÈME DE MENTHE
Ideal mouth-marriage match:
A mint dark chocolate

Prince Charles is partial to this drink. Personally, I'd keep a healthy distance as I'd never touch anything that resembles an infection. But if you really insist on drinking it, combine it with a high quality mint dark chocolate.

RUM

Ideal mouth-marriage match:

Milk chocolate

The one occasion I'll suggest milk chocolate is with rum. Although good luck finding a decent milk chocolate as most are just sweet milky fat that looks rather like liposuction extracts. Eat in moderation to avoid a chocolate hangover and chocolate over hang.

WINE

Ideal mouth-marriage match:

Cheese

Yes, cheese. I wouldn't combine wine with chocolate, other than the sweet dessert wines mentioned above. The cocoa beans just fight with the grapes. It's like Jordan and Peter André in your mouth and together they leave a bit of a nasty aftertaste.

> One of the world's best master chocolatiers is Paul A. Young, whose products are all handmade on the premises from the finest natural ingredients on the planet. He painstakingly sources all his materials and produces the most amazing chocolates to the highest specifications and

is beyond reproach in quality and perfection. As a lover of fine chocolate, I keep a fresh supply at home and it's always been a major triumph at the dinner table.

You can buy all of the chocolates mentioned here and more on line from him at: www.paulayoung.co.uk He has rather an encyclopedic knowledge of chocolate, so if you're planning a party and want to ask him direct what to serve chocolate wise, tweet him @paul_a_young for instant year-round guidance.

RECIPES:

Happily, Paul has developed a rather spectacularly desirable Positive Chocolate Martini for us all to enjoy. I have a bottle mulching in the fridge as I type and can confirm it's glorious.

CHOCOLATE MARTINI

1 litre bottle (or thereabouts) of premium vodka
200g cocoa nibs (roasted cracked cocoa beans which can be bought direct from chocolate specialists)
1 bottle cream soda
ice

You will need the bottle of vodka to be two-thirds full, add the cocoa nibs through a funnel into the bottle and shake well. Then simply shake every day for one month to help with the infusion, and leave for another week to settle. Once ready, take one large glass full of ice, pour slowly from the bottle a measure as required and fill to the top with cream soda.

'What you see before you, my friend, is the result of a lifetime of chocolate.'
Katharine Hepburn

PREHAB

'A hangover is the wrath of grapes.'
Anon

'I told you. Never drink the wine punch.'
Cleo Rocos

FAQ: Am I overdoing it?

Well, let's try a quiz and see.

Would you tick yes to any of the following?

☐ You deliberately re-carpeted your entire house in shag-pile carpet because it is easier to hang onto when lying on the floor.

☐ On the paint colour chart your eyes match the 'sunset yellow' estate emulsion.

☐ When you empty your dishwasher the glass-to-plate ratio is about ten to one.

☐ You lie to your cleaner that you 'had friends' round last night.

☐ If you shake your recycling bins the main noise they make is a clink.

☐ Winos and beggars do not ask you for money in the street. Instead they give you a nod of recognition and shuffle along the pavement to make space.

☐ You woke up this morning attached to a hospital drip.

☐ You woke up this morning attached to a policeman.

☐ You don't quite recollect being introduced to the person sharing your duvet.

☐ Supermarket staff smile and tell you to 'enjoy your party' as you leave the store. Yet you are actually planning a quiet evening in alone.

☐ The opening scene to *Leaving Las Vegas* looks really familiar.

☐ The last photo session you did was a police mug shot.

☐ You plan to complain to the publisher about all the blurred text in this book.

Listen. Have you thought of putting a cork in it for a month? I hear that rehab's no fun at all. Well, actually, I suppose it may have its moments. Quite a few Hollywood stars check in and confess to all sorts of naughty capers. *Breakfast at Tiffany's* star Patricia Neal once told me how she arrived at a clinic and walked straight into an AA meeting to support a family member. Now, never being one to let a good audience go to waste, she stood up and with a flourish, raised her hand, and addressed the group saying, 'My name is Patricia Neal and people say I am an alcoholic . . . But I'm NOT.' She always displayed a most wonderful and mischievous sense of humour. Needless to say the AA-goers found her visit a total joy and had a hilarious time meeting the Hollywood legend.

But you don't always get an A-lister to cheer things up, and in all seriousness I'd prefer to take you to **Prehab** so you will not end up in rehab. Slow things down before it gets to the stage of the bobsleigh hurtling towards the point of no return.

There's no harm in partying. There's no harm in a good night out. But this book is about positive drinking, and to drink positively you should always aim for two or three days away from alcohol each week so as to give the liver time to revitalise and to stay healthy. If you struggle to remember your last alcohol-free day, it may be time to throttle back a touch. Just a touch. Perhaps for a month? It is so easy. Just to give everything a rest. The beauty of stopping for a while is that when you take your first sip after a break, everything works to full effect and starts dancing around your palate with sheer delight. To appreciate drinking, you need to stop drinking sometimes.

As my lovely TV doctor friend and resident *This Morning* medic, Dr Chris Steele MBE, says: 'If you're drinking daily and your consumption is increasing your tolerance increases so you need more alcohol to produce the same effects and that can be a dangerous road to go down.'

That couple of days off each week just helps reset the whole thing: 'Your liver is the organ that breaks down the alcohol and it does have a remarkable ability to recover and repair itself – that's why you need drink-free days.'

Putting the brakes on stops drinking tipping over from being a pleasure into dependence. So those alcohol-free days are crucial, but they should still be savoured stylishly. There's no reason to curb your celebrations just because you're limited on libations.

> **FAQ:** Everyone talks about you if you're not drinking. They always assume you're ill, pregnant or weird. How can I go to a party, not drink, not let anyone know, and still have a good time?

'Water, taken in moderation, cannot hurt anybody.'
Mark Twain

The problem at some events is that it's always seen as almost insulting to the host to have anyone teetotal attending the party. Waft around with an orange juice or water in your hand and you're likely to come in for a great deal of questioning. A great trick that I know a lot of businessmen and women in the catering and hotel business use when they need a night off the drink, is to cheat and drink my 'Pink Gin' – not a real pink gin, but one that looks just like one, and magically seems to give you the same sort of kick. Well, maybe more of a little pinch. Whatever, it certainly won't send you reeling. I was first introduced to this clever little recipe by the impeccably elegant, flamboyantly witty and altogether splendid David Morgan-Hewitt, Managing Director of the Goring Hotel in London, which hosted Kate Middleton on the night before her wedding.

It's a drink that looks and tastes exactly like a refreshing cocktail, but leaves you as sober as a judge.

FAKE PINK GIN

1 small bottle tonic water (something delicious like Fever-Tree
for a proper taste)
3 drops Angostura bitters
1 slice of fresh lime or lemon

There will be a minute amount of alcohol in this as the bitters are a tincture. But it's only the merest hint of a drop. I quietly inform the barman at the start of the night that this is what I wish to drink, and that whenever he is asked for 'Cleo's pink gin' that's what he's to concoct. That way I can thoroughly enjoy the party season and go out every night whilst still keeping some nights alcohol free.

Make up a jug of this at dinner parties. Freeze some raspberries and add them to the mix. Serve it to drivers or non-drinkers and they won't feel left out. In fact, if you put a jug of this on the table at a dinner, I tend to find drinking guests drink roughly half the amount of wine they normally do, as they often ask what's in the mix, find it delicious, and drink glasses of this in between wine or champagne rounds.

Even if you go on the wagon for a bit, there's no need to give up shrieking and partying.

George W. Bush gave up alcohol after a particularly vigorous birthday weekend. Here's one non-alcoholic recipe, devised by a White House pastry chef.

WEST-WINGING-IT MOCKTAIL

1 litre still mineral water
2 lemon verbena stems
5 fresh mint leaves
3 tablespoons honey

Bring mineral water to a boil, remove from heat and then add lemon
verbena, mint and honey. Infuse for ten minutes, then strain.
Cool and serve over ice.

A LEGENDARY NIGHT OFF THE HARD STUFF

I had some quite wonderful evenings at Elizabeth Taylor's
house in Bel Air, Los Angeles. She'd invite her Hollywood
chums round for dinner and serve up plates of lovely food
and champagne for the guests. I especially loved the little
silver onions and potatoes with cream.

Elizabeth herself never drank anything stronger than
water. In fact, she had not had any alcohol for years. But
being a woman on the wagon did not stop her inviting
people round for wonderful parties and she was a huge
inspiration that the fun and partying needn't stop even if
you choose not to drink for a while. Don't lock yourself
away, carry on partying.

I remember some lovely evenings. Some of which revolved around her completely wacky adorable parrot called Marvin. One evening I arrived to find Elizabeth bathing Marvin in the kitchen sink. Between shrieks of laughter from both her and the parrot, she explained that Marvin had demanded she start bathing him 'via his therapist'.

I'll rewind as that sentence may take a bit of explaining. Marvin had 'issues' at this point; he wasn't behaving normally and seemed a little distressed. He just wasn't as happy a parrot as he had been and she knew it. So Elizabeth, being a massive animal lover, took him to see a pet therapist. Marvin squawked a bit and looked generally distracted as the therapist quizzed him. Then the therapist declared that he had spoken to her in 'parrot' and she understood his problems. She solemnly declared that Marvin 'wasn't happy with the ways thing have been going recently', that he wasn't entirely happy 'with the new maid', and the only thing that would make his parroty life take a turn for the better would be a nice bath in the kitchen sink. And, insisted the pet therapist as Elizabeth sat and listened intently: 'Marvin wants me to tell you that he wants you to do the bathing.'

So Marvin got his baths. Elizabeth would cackle joyously like a naughty witch, and insist that: 'he loves his baths', and Marvin would cackle like a witch after her.

> They were some of the best and relaxed dinner parties.
> And she was the most generous and gracious hostess.

So if you're temporarily off the sauce, don't worry, just get on with it and go with the flow. You don't need to consume great amounts of alcohol to enjoy yourself, just get high on the company. Just cackle like Marvin, flap your wings a bit, and carry on partying.

If you're preparing a non-alcoholic drink, you can make the whole thing look more decadent and fabulous by adding beautiful ice cubes. Here are a couple of recipes.

SUSPENDED FLOWERS IN ICE

Use edible flowers for a beautiful-looking drink that can add a lovely touch to a teetotal cocktail for non-drinkers.

Work in layers, fill a quarter of each ice cube space with mineral water. Add one flower facing downwards, and then freeze. Then fill to the top and freeze again.

ROSE ICE

As above, but add washed rose petals to the ice.

FROZEN FRUIT

A quick alternative is to throw fruit such as raspberries and grapes into the freezer, freeze and use as ice cubes. These work beautifully in the fake pink gin.

DIGESTIF

HOW NOT TO TRIP UP OVER A TIP

Tipping etiquette varies around the globe. Here's a handy cut out and keep guide to avoid any misunderstandings when drinking abroad.

AMSTERDAM

A tip is not expected. If you wish to round it up or leave a few small coins it will be appreciated, though. There are so many customers smoking exotic cigarettes out there that not many even remember.

ARGENTINA

Don't pay for me Argentina. Or rather do. If a service charge is not already there, a ten per cent tip is considered polite.

AUSTRALIA

Perhaps in the more upmarket restaurants leave no more than ten per cent if service was excellent, but generally there's no need to tip.

BARBADOS

Service will normally be added to a bill in a restaurant, if not add ten to fifteen per cent. When out drinking, if the Bajan rum stopped you from being glum give the bartender around $1 per round of drinks.

CANADA

If you drank Canada dry, then you should tip at between fifteen to twenty per cent, although larger groups may already have service added onto the bill.

CHINA

No need to tip. Actually, they find it offensive, which is handy when budgets are tight on a big night out.

FIJI

No need to tip. So have yourself an extra round.

FRANCE

The bill will tend to come with a service charge of fifteen per cent already on and the prices quoted on the menu usually include this charge. The restaurant will take this service charge but if your waiter has been excellent, line his pocket directly with, say, an extra ten per cent.

GERMANY

Your tip should be around fifteen per cent of your restaurant or bar bill, *danke schön*.

GREECE

If you frequent the bars for your meze and ouzos, then tip well with your euros – between ten and fifteen per cent and give it directly in cash to the waiter.

ITALY

If your Italian gives a stallion service please tip around ten per cent.

JAPAN

The land of the rising sun but not the rising bill. No need to tip.

MEXICO

To keep the man serving the Margarita that bit sweeter you should tip around ten to fifteen per cent. Tip in dollars preferably, but not coins.

SOUTH AFRICA

If you've enjoyed a nice daiquiri after your safari then in a restaurant or bar it's polite to tip between ten and fifteen per cent. But if service charge is already included there's no need to add extra.

SOUTH KOREA

Don't tip the servers. And don't point at any dogs on the premises either. Unless you fully understand the language and can explain perfectly what you mean by doggy bag.

SPAIN

No real need in a bar, but a five to ten per cent is a good guide for a higher level of restaurant.

SWITZERLAND

Service is included on the menu already. Again, if service was excellent you can add a little thank-you on top. Say, five to ten per cent.

TURKEY

Tip between five and ten per cent on your bar or restaurant bill. But you have to leave the tip in cash, rather than add it to your bill, so take some extra notes. And leave notes, as foreign change cannot be converted into Turkish lira. Do not use Turkish notes from pre 2008 as most places will not accept them.

UK

In a restaurant ask if the bill includes service. If it does and you wish to tip over this for excellent service, then go ahead. There's no need to tip in bars.

USA

The serving staff will be reliant on your tip for a wage so if you don't tip they really don't like it and are liable to let you know. Pay fifteen per cent, which is normal for both bars and restaurants, and around twenty per cent for exceptional service in a full service restaurant.

HOW TO GET WHAT YOU PLEASE WHEN DRINKING OVERSEAS

USEFUL PHRASES

It's no use drinking positively at home, if the second you go abroad you let it all slide. So here are some handy phrases to help you cope with round-the-world drinking.

In Spanish, German and Chinese (and phonetic Chinese as the alphabet's tricky to master).

Get me to a Margarita And there's a guinea in it for you.

(E) Póngame una margarita. Y le doy a usted un par de euros.

(D) Führen Sie mich zu einem Margarita. Da sind ein paar Euro für Sie drin.

(CN) 幫我拿杯margarita來, 這裡有幾兩銀子給你!

Bang wo na bei Margarita lai... Zhe li you ji liang yin zi gei ni!

Where do I get a decent Martini round here?

(E) ¿Dónde ponen un martini decente por aquí?

(D) Wo bekommt man hier einen anständigen Martini?

(CN) 這兒哪裡有像樣的Martini?

Zhe er na li you xiang yan de Martini?

Open the bar, would you, my good man?

(E) Vamos… abra ya el bar, buen hombre.

(D) Machen Sie doch bitte die Bar für mich auf, guter Mann.

(CN) 開一下吧檯,掌櫃的!

Kai yi xia ba tai, zhang gui de!

Barking for a large one, it's been a hell of a day.

Ⓕ Me muero por una grande. Vaya día que he tenido.

Ⓓ Ich kann jetzt einen gebrauchen. Ich hab' einen höllischen Tag hinter mir.

ⒸⓃ 今天可累死我啦,給我一個超大杯的.

　　Jin tian ke lei se wo la! Gei wo yi ge chao da bei de.

Can't you pour it any faster?

Ⓔ ¿No la puede servir más rápido?

Ⓓ Können Sie denn nicht schneller einschenken?

ⒸⓃ 可不可以倒快點?

　　Ke bu ke yi dao kuai dian?

Keep them coming . . .

Ⓔ Venga, que no paren…

Ⓓ Schenken Sie mal ruhig nach …

ⒸⓃ 今天不醉不歸...酒繼續來...

　　Jin tian bu zui bu gui... Jiu ji xu lai...

Is it twenty-four-hour room service?

Ⓔ ¿Hay servicio de habitación las 24 horas?

Ⓓ Gibt es hier Zimmerservice rund um die Uhr?

ⒸⓃ 這客房服務是二十四小時的嗎?

　　Zhe ke fang fu wu shi er shi si xiao shi de ma?

The barman will need to be at full throttle on his mixing ability for us.

(E) El camarero tendrá que estar en plena forma e ir a todo gas para servirnos.

(D) Der Barmann soll beim Mixen für uns aber Gas geben.

(CN) 酒保調酒能力今天都要拿出來喔!

Jiu bao tiao jiu neng li jin tian dou yao na chu lai o!

Why did I drink that punch last night? Could you fix me a Bloody Mary?

(E) ¿Por qué bebería esa copa anoche? ¿Me pone un bloody mary por favor?

(D) Warum habe ich letzte Nacht nur diesen Punsch getrunken? Geben Sie mir bitte einen Bloody Mary.

(CN) 我昨天為什麼要那酒呢? 幫我弄一杯血腥瑪麗好嗎?

Wo zuo tian wei shen me yao he jiu ne? Bang wo nong yi bei Xie Xing Ma Li hao ma?

I'd like you to order me a cab to arrive in two Margaritas' time, please.

(E) Pídame un taxi y que me dé tiempo a dos margaritas.

(D) Bestellen Sie mir bitte ein Taxi, aber lassen Sie mir noch Zeit für zwei Margaritas.

(CN) 我要你幫我叫一輛車來 ， 兩杯 margarita以後到就差不多.

Wo yao ni bang wo jiao yi liang che lai, liang bei margarita yi hou dao jiu cha bu duo.

I'll throw my last scruple to the wind and order another.

(E) Ya me da igual y pido otra.

(D) Jetzt ist mir alles egal und ich bestelle noch einen.

(CN) 算了!我豁出去了!再給我一杯吧!

Suan le! Wo huo chu qu le! Zai gei wo yi bei ba!

I'm currently suffering somewhat of a financial embarrassment.
Could you possibly see me clear for this bar bill?

(E) He de confesarle que no tengo un duro.... ¿No me podría usted

zanjar de la cuenta del bar por casualidad?

(D) Ich bin finanziell leider in einer peinlichen Lage. Könnten Sie

vielleicht die Barrechnung für mich begleichen?

(CN) 我現在經濟上有困難,你可以把單免了嗎?

Wo xian zai jing ji shang you kun nan. Ni ke yi ba dan mian le

ma?

THE AFTERMATH

FAQ: I did not drink positively last night. I've learned my lesson and won't be going to that person's parties ever again. In the meantime, is there anything, anything at all that can help me?

Having followed the rules of this book, none of this should be needed. However, in case of emergency, I bring you the ideal hangover breakfast.

If you can't face the science bit right now just go straight to the recipes.

THE SCIENCE BIT

Your hangover is being caused by the alcohol being broken down into an enzyme called alcohol dehydrogenase into a by-product called acetaldehyde. As Dr David Bull explains: 'Acetaldehyde is ten to thirty times more toxic to the body than alcohol itself.' And that's what is making you feel so sick right now.

Added to that, the body then works at converting this into acetic acid, but as Dr Bull adds: 'This compound stops the body from producing glucose so the blood glucose falls.'

In addition to this, if you haven't followed my advice on avoiding additives, then you're in even more trouble as: 'Any additives to the drinks, like sugars or different compounds, produce by-products like methanol. This is converted to a very toxic chemical called formaldehyde, which causes ketoacidiosis, which means the body becomes very acidic.' Methanol is also a by-product of poor distillation techniques, so if you didn't follow my advice on selecting the purest spirit available, that's what's going on inside you right now.

Alcohol will also have affected your kidneys, making them less efficient at recycling water, so it will have caused dehydration.

Worry not, for help is at hand. Let's tackle the causes one by one, following Dr Bull's advice and see what will help.

Dehydration: The kidneys will have suffered so make sure you rehydrate well. Drink lots of fluids. The old chestnut of a glass of water before bed really does work if you can manage it.

Electrolytes: These will be severely depleted. Drinking sports drinks, dioralyte rehydration powders or coconut water will help.

Eggs: These contain a chemical called cysteine, which helps to restore normal function.

Milk Thistle: This seems to reduce nausea and helps to regenerate liver cells. It seems more effective when coupled with exposure to the sun (which makes Vitamin D), so take a pack on holiday and it will help things.

Brewer's Yeast: This contains vitamin B6 which can help to reduce the severity of a hangover. A study carried out by the Tulane University Health Sciences Center found that Vitamin B6 can help a hangover as it helps liver function, so take an extra supplement before and after drinking. Too high a dose, however, can be toxic, so limit your B6 supplement to 100mg.

N-Acetyl-Cysteine: Available as capsules or as powder to add to drinks. This reduces the level of the toxic product acetaldehyde. It is best when combined with Vitamin B1.

Ginger: This reduces nausea and the stomach upset.

Controversially . . .

Alcohol: This will block the production of the toxic chemical formaldehyde so many people swear by 'hair of the dog' to help.

Just one glass, though, please. If you reach for a bottle you're merely postponing your trip to hangover hell.

AN EMERGENCY BLOODY MARY FOR THOSE FEELING DISTINCTLY LESS THAN POSITIVE
25ml vodka

5ml dry sherry

2 dashes Angostura® aromatic bitters

50ml tomato juice

15ml lemon juice

4 drops Tabasco sauce

½ shot Worcestershire sauce
½ tsp horseradish sauce
GARNISH: Ground pepper and celery stick.

Shake and strain and consume horizontally.

More controversially still . . .

Cannabis: Only legal in some parts. But the active ingredient THC reduces the nausea and the headache. It also increases the appetite so that you eat, which counteracts the drop in blood sugar levels.

However, it also reduces you to a giggling fool, and, unless you're inside an Amsterdam café, this really is a risky option. The cocktails service inside UK jails, I believe, really isn't up to scratch.

One more act of salvation, and one that is a little more legally approved, comes from Dr John Emsley of the Royal Society of Chemistry who recommends a bacon sandwich and honey on toast.

Here comes his science behind the breakfast: 'You can help the enzymes that are removing alcohol and acetaldehyde by providing fructose. This simple sugar is not directly involved but it produces a chemical called NAD (short for nicotinamide adenine dinucleotide), which the enzymes need. Foods rich in fructose are honey and jam so a breakfast of toast and honey should help.

'If drinking has caused the body to lose too much water, and with it salt, then breakfasting on a bacon sandwich should help.'

And that, scientifically speaking, is all I can really offer you in your hour of need. You will just have to let things run their course and I suggest a lie-down in a darkened room until it all goes away.

Buy last night's hosts a copy of this book and ask them to serve you something decent next time. If you follow this book you should never, ever, have to look at this chapter again.

Happy drinking.

'Death is a natural part of life. Rejoice for those around you who transform into the Force.'

Yoda, Star Wars Episode III: Revenge of the Sith

'What a marvellous thought, you wise little thing. I think that's worth a celebratory glass.'

Cleo Rocos

Once you've mastered the Power of Positive Drinking, being with us only in spirit need be no barrier to having a good time.

Billy Wilder once told me about an underground poker-and-whisky club from the glory days of Hollywood attended by the likes of Mae West, Douglas Fairbanks and Alan Ladd and a few others who would get together once a week from their various studios and swap all the raucous gossip. The American comedian and writer W. C. Fields, who was known to be rather fond of a drink or two, was a founder member of the weekly poker game and a leading light of the drinking crew. When he passed away in 1946, as a mark of respect at their next gathering the poker players laid him a place at the table, poured him a whisky as usual, and dealt the cards for him.

It was a couple of rounds of poker and a bottle of whisky later that everyone realised quite how much they missed W. C. Fields – far too much to be able to carry on without him. So they broke into the funeral parlour where he'd been prepared for burial the next day.

They lifted the body, carried him to their poker game, sat him up, put a whisky in his hand and carried on the game before drunkenly returning the body.

This is the ultimate tribute to a fellow party pal. I have asked my friends to do exactly the same for me when I go. This is why I never go out in public wearing beige or without my lipstick. If I ever get killed I want to be ready and looking spectacular just in case there's one more cocktail session to be had.

STOCKISTS

Amathus Drinks: www.amathusdrinks.com

Amazon: www.amazon.co.uk

AquaRiva Tequilas: www.aquariva.co.uk

Cambridge Wine Merchants: www.cambridgewine.com

Chocolate: Paul A. Young: www.paulayoung.co.uk

Duty Free: Virgin Atlantic Airlines www.retailtherapyshopping.com

Drake & Morgan Restaurants/Bars London www.drakeandmorgan.co.uk

Eskimo Ice Deliveries: www.eskimo-ice.co.uk

Fentiman's tonic water: www.fentimans.com

Fever-Tree Tonic Water: www.fever-tree.com

Gerry's: www.gerrys.uk.com

Harvey Nichols: www.harveynichols.com

Majestic Wine glass loans: www.majestic.co.uk/Freeglass loan

Portobello Road Gin and Ginstitute: www.portobellostarbar.co.uk

Sainsbury's: www.sainsburys.co.uk

Soho Wine Supply: www.sohowine.co.uk

The Drink Shop: www.thedrinkshop.com

The Vodka Emporium: www.vodkaemporium.com

The Whisky Exchange: www.thewhiskyexchange.com

Waitrose: www.waitrose.com

And I'm here to help in drinking emergencies:

cleo@POPD.co.uk
   or follow
@cleorocos1 on twitter.

ABOUT THE AUTHOR

C leo Rocos is the essential ingredient to any party that wants to go with a swing, and has spent a lifetime partying with the best of them, as a host of bon viveurs from Elizabeth Taylor and Princess Diana to Alan Carr and Gore Vidal would attest. She is also an international spirits judge.

When she competed in Britain's Best Celebrity Chef in March 2009 she won over the judges and audience with her Mexican cooking and Margaritas. Her love for Mexico and its favourite drink has led to her adoption by the tequila industry, where she has been honoured by its official governing body. 2012 saw her launching her own brand of 100 per cent agave tequila, AquaRiva, with high-profile lifestyle brand partners such as Virgin Atlantic, Waitrose and Sainsbury's. Working with a top master blender in Mexico to achieve her exact specifications, it has already won many top international awards, including Best of the Best in the world's biggest competition held by tequila.net. She has also launched her own award-winning AquaRiva organic agave syrup.

Cleo's life has always been something of a party. She was born in Rio de Janeiro to Greek and English parents. After a first job as a professional skateboarder, her career in television and comedy took off when she co-starred in *The Kenny Everett Show* on BBC1, starting in the 1980s – then the number-one rated comedy series in the UK. It ran for eight years, immortalising Everett's infamously zany, anarchic and saucy comedy.

Following her early work in the original *Hitchhiker's Guide to the Galaxy* and as a roving reporter for *That's Life!*, she has worked between the UK and the US for a range of broadcasters including the BBC, ITV, Channel Four, Channel Five and NBC, and co-starred with names ranging from Emma Thompson and Rhys Ifans to Roger Daltrey and Leigh Francis.

Cleo's one-woman show in Los Angeles was a sell-out hit with star-studded audiences, followed by a one-woman show in London's Soho. She has also duetted with Marc Almond live at the Royal Albert Hall. Her autobiography *Bananas Forever: Kenny and Me*, covering her years working with Kenny Everett, was published in 1998.

She produced *The Seven Year Itch* starring Darryl Hannah at the Queen's Theatre in London's West End, and produced and presented the hit TV series *Cleo Worldwide* for Channel 5 with guests including Neil Morrissey, Denise van Outen, Terry Venables, Julian Clary, Tessa Dahl, Nicky Haslam and Lord Glenconner. She was also Executive Producer of the Comic Strip's film *Sex Actually* for Channel 4, featuring Rik Mayall and Sheridan Smith.

Cleo starred as herself in Channel 4's *Celebrity Big Brother* in 2007 alongside Jermaine Jackson and Ken Russell. She has also presented several travel special reports for *This Morning*, and appeared on *Celebrity Come Dine with Me* in Autumn 2011.

Cleo Rocos lives in London, the party city of the world.

ACKNOWLEDGEMENTS

A throbbingly huge thank you to my brilliant literary agent, the most talented, witty and divinely eloquent Gordon Wise. Also a massive thank you to the fabulous Rosemary Davidson and her most glamourous and talented team. No words can describe the utter joy of working with the beautiful Sharon Marshall; an immensely skilled and creative wordsmith. A big thank you also to all supporters and key experts which include Stuart Freeman, Kyri Sotiri, Ivan Dixon, Jake Burger, Dr David Bull, Dr Chris Steele, Drake and Morgan group, and Paul A. Young. And to Virgin Atlantic for being the first to serve AquaRiva tequila No Hangover Margaritas.

INDEX